September 9, 201
Santa (Rosa) - Cloveda, California

Dear Momma Mielle! (It's late 7:10PM ☺)
Welcome Home from Australia!!
Jaden, Carson, and Tommy are delightful,
busy, smart, busy, creative, funny, busy and
love each other and their Mom and
dad. They have missed you and cried for you. In your
"package" came the gift for nurturing
and teaching children. I
honor and respect you for magnifying this
gift —
With tears,
Mom

Great
Kids Are
Homemade

Written by Shelley Wille

Illustrated by Craig Harris

Shelley Wille majored in Family Life Education. She is an author, lecturer, homemaker, and mother of six children.

Dr. Craig Harris attended school at the University of North Carolina, and the University of Washington. He currently is a professor at the University of Michigan.

Library of Congress Catalog Card Number: 99-95540
ISBN 0-9674553-0-8

Printed in the United States by Publishers Press, Salt Lake City, Utah

Table of Contents

Get Organized!

Everyone knows how essential planning and organizing are to be successful in anything! As a parent, if you are to accomplish your goals of building a close, loving family in an atmosphere where great kids can develop and thrive, it will take some real organization or you will be spinning your wheels doing things that are of less value. Take a careful look at your priorities...are you making time to do the things that really matter the most?

We must go beyond just taking care of the bare essentials of feeding and clothing our children. We must be actively involved in loving, training, and teaching our children!

As a parent you can't build a close family, and influence your children for the good, if your children are never home. The only way to compete with a child's friends and their interest in activities outside of the home, is to offer them something which will make them want to be home more than they want to be somewhere else. This usually doesn't just happen--it takes some effort and serious planning on your part.

If you take the time to plan, and then carry out, fun activities that bring a greater feeling of closeness and growth to your family, you will have achieved something truly great!

Have a planning meeting (with yourself) once a week. A good time to do this might be on Sunday evening after all has become quiet. This is the time to plan the Friday night family activity, the weekly children's "date with Dad" activity, and any other responsibilities for which you need to prepare as well as personal goals for the week. This can often be accomplished in less than an hour. It will keep you from having to push the panic button when it's time for your weekly family activity and you have absolutely nothing planned. If you are unprepared, your activity will flop and the children's enthusiasm for future family activities will quickly fade.

There are usually four, and occasionally five, Friday nights in a month. Reserve this night of the week for activities with the family. Most of these family activities are quick and easy to plan and prepare. Here are some sample activities you might want to plan:

Service Activity...

To teach your children the joy of serving takes some thoughtful pre-planning. Children who don't learn to serve will grow up to be selfish and self-centered adults. Serving others is something that is best taught at home through the example of loving parents. Choose one service project a month to carry out as a family and then watch the growth take place in each family member as they learn to put the needs of others above their own!

Video Night...

Don't rent videos during a week night, or even on a regular basis on weekends, or this will ruin the fun of video night! Only rent once a month! Choose great videos to watch as a family and don't forget the popcorn or chips and salsa. Wrap up in blankets, snack a bit, and enjoy a great movie as a family together.

Entertaining...

I think it is so important to occasionally invite other families over to your house, even if it is only for dinner and some time spent visiting after the meal. If you open your home up to others, and show interest and love, you will teach your children to open their lives to others as well as teach them many skills and lessons. For example, they will learn how to be a good host or hostess; they can be taught table manners and etiquette; and they will learn how to act appropriately around, and how to get along with, others. It's fun to have a new family over once a month!

I have tried for years to be creative and to fix something new and exciting each time we have had a family over for dinner. However, the fear and anxiety of preparing a dish that somebody might not like would often cause me to dread, rather than look forward to, guests coming over. So what do I do now? Simple--I fix spaghetti and meat sauce, green salad and dressing, a frozen vegetable, and French garlic bread. For dessert, I serve ice cream. This is a quick and easy meal to make, which everyone seems to like. This takes the pressure off me so that I can then relax and enjoy the meal and the rest of the evening along with everyone else!

Invite others into your home--reach out and touch other people's lives!

Outside Activity Night...

Our communities offer many activities for us to enjoy as a family. We enjoy attending school and community concerts, high school and college plays, or simply a great movie at the local theater. Then, of course, there are church activities to look forward to, swimming together as a family, or attendance at high school basketball and football games! If your community offers it, you might occasionally wish to go bowling or miniature golfing together. This is an opportunity you have to let your children broaden their interests and to be culturally well-rounded in music, dance, sports, etc. Take advantage of every opportunity and save your money for these types of experiences!

Family Activity Night...

The following pages are filled with tons of ideas for you to use for family activity night. Many of these can also be adapted for other special occasions, such as birthdays or for group dating by your teenagers. Some of these ideas revolve around food and fun, some are quick and easy to do, and others are more involved party bashes! Have a great time trying these and watch your children's faces light up as you surprise them with an evening full of fun spent together as a family!

At the Dinner Table

Food and fun just naturally seem to go together! You have to fix a meal every evening anyway--so why not "spice things up" every now and then by adding a little fun to the menu? Here are a few ideas you might want to try....

BARBARIAN DINNER

Tell family members that you are planning a very special evening meal. Give them a specific hour and tell them you would like them to be on time. As they arrive, hand them an old shirt or apron to put on over their clothes. Ask them to be seated.

Prepare for this meal in advance by covering your table with a plastic tablecloth or with disposable paper. Place only glasses or mugs on the table--no silverware, plates, or napkins. Cover the table, including the glasses with a sheet or blanket. Remove the sheet or blanket and begin to bring out the food. For the most fun, try using this menu: spaghetti and meat sauce, green salad with dressing, French bread, spinach or corn, and chocolate ice cream for dessert.

Begin serving each family member by walking around the table behind them, stopping to plop down a heap of spaghetti on the table in front of them. Follow this up by placing spaghetti sauce on top. Continue by serving each item on the menu, dropping it on the table in front of them. They must eat their meal barbarian style, using only their fingers--no forks or spoons allowed! Now the fun begins! Don't forget to break out the chocolate ice cream...and the camera for pictures!

PIZZA UNDER THE STARS

Pick a warm summer evening when the sky is clear and the moon is full. Then surprise your family with a late night picnic under the stars. Earlier in the evening feed the family a light and easy meal for dinner--soup or peanut butter sandwiches. (Be certain that everyone goes to bed moaning about being hungry!) Once it's dark and the children have been in bed for a few minutes, go out in the back yard and throw a blanket out on the grass (or on the trampoline, if you have one). Order a pizza over the phone. When it arrives, have the children get up and put on a jacket. Lead them outside to the blanket. Enjoy pizza and pop, observe falling stars, and (using a Boy Scout handbook) point out constellations.

MYSTERY MEAL

Sit everyone at the table with a plate and glass in front of him or her. Hand each a pencil and a menu that you have prepared beforehand. There should be twenty items listed on the menu and each person is to mark their menu, indicating which items they wish served to them during each of the 4 courses. They should place a "1" beside five of the items on the menu for the first course, a "2" beside five others they choose, and so on until they have place a 1, 2, 3, or 4 next to each item.

Take the menus from them and begin serving each person the first course as he or she has indicated. By not knowing what they have ordered they might, for example, end up with corn on their plate but no fork to eat it with. Be certain to remove all items from one course before serving the next--leave only the plate and glass. Here is a sample menu for you:

(1) Latte (milk)
(2) Pane (bread)
(3) Forchetta (fork)
(4) Minestra (soup)
(5) Carota (carrot)
(6) Carne panino (meat loaf)
(7) Insalata (salad)
(8) Patata (potato)
(9) Coltello (knife)
(10) Pomodor (tomato slice)

(11) Sottaceto (pickle)
(12) Petardo (cracker)
(13) Stuzzicadenti (toothpick)
(14) Callo (corn)
(15) Burro (butter)
(16) Marmellata (jam)
(17) Sedano (celery)
(18) Sugo (juice)
(19) Cucchiaio (spoon)
(20) Dolce (dessert)

SILLY SUPPER

Prepare a meal that will require the use of a knife, fork, and spoon. For example: meat, baked potato, salad, soup, and bread and butter. Also prepare a paper bag for each family member, placing inside the bag those utensils that they will use to eat this meal. Rather than using normal knives, forks, spoons, plates and glasses, here are some items you might use instead…

In place of silverware: potato masher, manual can opener, ice cream scoop, 1/4 teaspoon measuring spoon, pizza cutter, spatula, etc.

In place of dish or plate: quart canning jar, small measuring cup, muffin tin, large mixing bowl, cookie sheet, etc.

In place of a glass: baby bottle, blender, large pitcher, gravy bowl, etc.

Have each person choose a bag without seeing its contents. No substitutions are allowed--they must eat their meal using the equipment in their own bag.

ORIENTAL FUN FEAST

Bring out your Wok, your chopsticks, and your favorite oriental menu, such as, chow mein, fried rice, egg rolls, and fortune cookies. Chopsticks can be purchased at party shops.

If time is limited, these oriental foods can be purchased already prepared in the can, ready to heat up, with the exception of fried rice (substitute with Rice-a-roni).

Set the mood by playing oriental background music that can be obtained and checked out from your local public library. Prepare your meal using your Wok. Sit on pillows and eat on a low-to-the-ground, oriental-type table. Either use your coffee table or construct a table by using boards, plywood, or a door on top of cinder blocks or bricks. This meal might take the whole evening to eat, since there is no cheating...chopsticks *must* be used. And, of course, don't forget to read your fortunes!

SOUTH OF THE BORDER

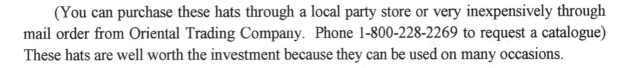

Purchase a Mexican hat (sombrero) for each family member.

(You can purchase these hats through a local party store or very inexpensively through mail order from Oriental Trading Company. Phone 1-800-228-2269 to request a catalogue) These hats are well worth the investment because they can be used on many occasions.

Check out some Spanish music from your local library and play it in the background to set the mood. Together as a family, prepare a wonderful Mexican meal. Some menu possibilities could include tacos, nachos and dip, taco salad, burritos, etc.

For activities, begin by improvising your own Mexican hat dance. Simply place a hat on the ground, divide in pairs, face each other, join hands and hop on your left foot while kicking with the right foot. Then reverse and hop on right while kicking with left. At the chorus, hook right arms together and skip around the hat.

Next watch *The Three Amigos* on video. Then take the family out to the back yard. While outside, hang a candy-filled Piñata on a tree or swing set, and then take turns trying to break it. (This will also act as your dessert!) Be sure to use a plastic bat and to blindfold the family member who is swinging it. Watch for sales on Piñatas. You can often buy one for only $5.00 if you shop around. They are well worth the fun!

HARVEST DINNER

Here's a great way to motivate your family to actually grow a thriving garden this summer. As you are planting in the spring, tell the family that at harvest time, you will be serving a special harvest dinner made up of those items you have grown in your garden...so plan your menu accordingly! For even greater motivation, halfway through the summer, send out invitations to family and friends to join in the harvest feast!

During the actual meal, set your table outside close to your garden--or, if you live out in the country, set up your table out in a field. Decorate your table using homegrown flowers. Possible menu ideas: pepper steak (uses green peppers and tomatoes), zucchini bread, corn on the cob, baked potatoes, carrot sticks, raspberry or strawberry JELL-O, sliced tomatoes (or tomato juice), etc. To add a little more atmosphere to the setting, decorate the area with a wheelbarrow, shovels, hoes, work gloves, and so forth.

FONDUE FEAST

If you have never had fondue before, this is something you really want to try. This is a super fun activity, which can be done several times a year. A fondue pot costs about $20 or watch for these at garage sales and you can get them for much less. You will probably need about three of them. This is a great investment, which is well worth the initial cost.

You can experiment with different recipes--but I like to do everything nice and easy. Simply warm up vegetable oil in one pot, cheddar cheese soup in another (add only 1/4 cup of water per can of soup), and either chocolate fudge or caramel ice cream topping in another fondue pot. There is a wonderful variety of food items which can be sliced or broken into bite-sized pieces and either cooked in the oil, or dipped in the cheese or chocolate.

In the oil, cook small pieces of steak, pre-cooked meatballs, scones (using Pillsbury rolls), French fries or tator tots. In the cheese, dip pieces of French bread, celery, cherry tomatoes, and fresh broccoli. In the chocolate, dip slices of bananas, apples, marshmallows, donut holes, and angel food cake. Stab each item and dip with fondue forks, which come with the pots. This is one messy meal--but boy is it fun!

BIKE-A-MEAL!

Prepare a fun picnic for your family--something as easy as submarine sandwiches, chips & dip, a summer finger food tray of veggies and fruit, and an easy dessert. Warn the family that they must go on a treasure hunt on their bikes in order to eat tonight!

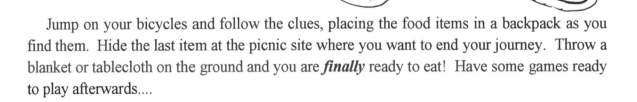

About an hour before the family bike ride, hide the five different food items noted above and the clues, which will be used to find them. Conceal them very well so that others who are NOT INVITED will not find and steal your meal! Use a friend's mailbox, the flower bed at the church, the limb of a tree, a friend's backyard, etc.

Jump on your bicycles and follow the clues, placing the food items in a backpack as you find them. Hide the last item at the picnic site where you want to end your journey. Throw a blanket or tablecloth on the ground and you are *finally* ready to eat! Have some games ready to play afterwards....

Another version of this type of activity is to hide about eight clues, which will lead you around town. The last clue tells everyone where you have hidden the picnic!

THE TWO BUCK MEAL DEAL

Sometimes you find yourself just plain tired of cooking and you need a little break from the kitchen. Next time that this happens, announce to everyone that the family is going to the grocery store for dinner tonight. Remind family members how they are always complaining about wanting to eat this or that for dinner, and this is their big chance to have whatever they want!

Give each person two dollars with which to buy whatever they want to eat. No one should know what the other family members are buying. Go back home and have each person prepare his or her part of the meal...and then sit down and eat!

A small note of warning: when our family tries this, our menu often consists of Lucky Charms, soda pop, ice cream, a beef stick, crackers & cheese, and cookies! It will probably make you feel better though, if you do your motherly duty and buy bananas and oranges to offset the junk!

A FAMILY PROGRESSIVE LAWN PARTY

Assign each family member a part of a picnic meal to prepare: a drink, a salad, a bread item, a main dish, a dessert, or a veggie and fruit plate. Tell them they must also select and make whatever preparations are necessary to play one game. Then go from child to child, eating the food they have prepared and playing the game, which they have chosen.

TAKING THE FAMILY "OUT" TO DINNER

Get the family excited by telling them you are going *out* to dinner. After every one is in the car, drive around for awhile, discussing places where you might like to eat. Then tell them you have a great idea. You know a place where they have never eaten before!

While you are driving around, by previous arrangement have some friends set up a table in your front yard. If this is too embarrassing for you, have the table set up in a local park near the street. The table should be covered with a nice table cloth, candles, etc. Assemble the family around you and tell them how excited you are to be eating "OUT" and explain that your meal will soon be delivered.

As previously arranged have two friends "deliver" the meal to you in their car. Give them the food that you want delivered and instruct them to drive by and throw one dinner item out the window to you about every five minutes.

As they drive by the first time, have them throw out a large, plastic Ziploc bag that contains plates, cups, plastic silverware and a note that says: "Here's your thrown together dinner!" On the next pass they will throw out the car window a "tossed" salad with a plastic jar of dressing.

As they speed by on subsequent runs they will deliver "Smashed Sandwiches" -- "Squished Chips" -- "Pitched Punch" -- with "Hurled Jell" for dessert. At the end of the meal, they will pass by and throw a game out of the window for you to play!

SATURDAY MORNING MADNESS

If you don't usually purchase highly sugared cold cereal and it's a real *treat* for your family to have some, buy two or three boxes of your children's favorite brands. Everyone can eat his or her favorite--or mix and match. Then spend the morning watching Saturday cartoons (or rent your favorite) with your children, relaxing, and wearing your pajamas until noon!

BACK TO THE FIFTIES BASH!

Have the family dress up 50's style! Girls wear pigtails or pony tails, skirts, white bobby socks, with the arms of a sweater tied around their neck. Boys wear rolled up blue jeans, white socks, hair slicked back, and white tee shirts with sleeves rolled. Get out your old rock 'n roll music from either the fifties or sixties (the kids won't know the difference). Just make sure it's the good old bebop music!

Begin your party by serving food from the fifties: hamburgers and French fries in a plastic basket (obtain baskets at the local dollar store) and rootbeer floats. Teach the family to dance the swing, the twist, the monkey, mashed potatoes, etc. Many libraries have videos on learning to dance, so if you yourself don't know how, it's time to learn!

Next, dust off the old ping pong table--or borrow a net, paddles, and ball from a neighbor and use the kitchen table. Play checkers, croquette, and then, as a grand finale, take your children to drag "Main" (remember driving up and down main street, waving at every one over and over again?). Of course, don't forget to explain to them what you are doing!

"PIG OUT" PARTY

Go to your local grocery store and purchase inexpensive tin casserole trays--or use wall paper trays--one for each member of the family. Use these as "troughs." Fix your family their favorite meal...lasagna, beef stroganoff, or spaghetti work really well! Fill the troughs and set them out on the table--everyone must eat dinner without using their hands, eating like pigs! Kids especially love watching Dad make a pig of himself!

After dinner, play pig games. One of our favorites is "Pass the Pig" (by Milton Bradley--you can purchase at your local toy store). Another is "Grunt, Piggy, Grunt!" To play this game have everyone sit in a circle. One person is chosen to begin the game and is blindfolded. Once he is blindfolded, everyone jumps up, moves to a new position in the circle, and then sits down. The blindfolded person reaches out, touches someone in the circle, and says "Grunt, Piggy, Grunt". The person who is touched then must "grunt" and "snort" like a pig. The blindfolded person then tries to guess who the "pig" is. If successful, the "pig" takes the place of the blindfolded person and the above-described process is repeated. If unsuccessful in correctly guessing who the "pig" is, the blindfolded person touches someone else, listens to the "grunts", and tries to guess who it is. You will find this game to be great fun!

SUMMER TIME PROGRESSIVE BREAKFAST

Once in awhile it's great fun to invite other families to do things with yours! On a Saturday during the summer invite two or three other families to join you on a progressive breakfast at the park! Have each family bring a Coleman stove, a tablecloth, and come prepared to provide and cook a part of the meal. Then go from table to table eating breakfast!

A fun and easy menu could be:

Family #1: Scrambled eggs
Family #2: Bacon or sausage
Family #3: Pancakes cooked on a big park grill
Family #4: Hashbrowns and juice

Take time to play with the children on the playground equipment and enjoy visiting with your friends. Pretty soon you'll be having so much fun that you will forget all about all of that yard work and gardening you have waiting for you back home!

SURPRISE BREAKFAST

As a family choose two other families that you would like to have over for food and fun! Inform the **wife** of each of these families that they are invited to breakfast at your home on a certain day and that you will be over to pick them up at 6:30 a.m. Swear her to secrecy, making certain that she will not tell any other family members of these plans.

Arrive at each home at the appointed hour and ring the doorbell. Take everyone to your house wearing their pajamas and bathrobes, without giving them time to comb their hair, brush their teeth, or put on make-up. Have breakfast all ready to eat when you arrive and get out the video camera!

KIDNAPPED FOR BREAKFAST

On a Saturday morning wake your children early and blindfold them using bandannas or dishtowels. For fun, as an added affect, you might want to tie their hands behind their backs! Walk them silently out to the car, not talking or telling them where you are taking them.

Drive around the neighborhood a little while they try to figure out where you are going. Then drive to a fun park and fix breakfast using your camp stove or a park grill. If you can't get your teenagers out of the car once they discover they will have to wear their pajamas in public, you might have to let them eat in the car! Ha! Another option would be to kidnap the children and take them to breakfast at a fast food restaurant. But be nice and let them get dressed first--or next time, YOU might be the one kidnapped!

A HAPPY MEAL

Early in the week, announce to the family that on Friday you will be having a "happy night." As part of the fun, each person should be prepared to tell several jokes or funny stories during the evening meal! They can obtain jokes from someone at school or from joke books at the library. They can also relate personal "embarrassing moment" stories if they wish. Friday evening have Dad bring home a McDonald's "Happy Meal" for each family member. While eating the meal picnic-style on the floor, take turns sharing your jokes. Be sure to laugh whether the jokes are very funny or not (or whether or not you even understand them)! There is nothing more fun than hearing children's laughter!

When dinner is over, play "the happy hanky." To do this, have the family sit in a circle on the family room floor. One person kneels in the middle of the circle and throws a handkerchief into the air. Immediately everyone in the circle starts laughing hysterically. But, when the hanky touches the floor everyone must be perfectly quiet. Anyone who is still laughing after the hanky lands must leave the circle and is out of the game for this round. The person in the middle then throws the hanky in the air again and everyone again starts laughing. Each person in the circle tries to act so funny or laugh so silly (while the hanky is in the air) that others in the circle will be caught still laughing when they are supposed to be quiet. The person throwing the hanky can also make funny faces at family members to try to make them laugh when they are supposed to be still. The last person left in the circle is the winner and gets to throw the hanky for the next round.

Complete the evening by watching a funny movie together. Either rent a comedy from the video store, or use your video camera and spend the evening writing, directing, and acting out a comedy movie of your own!

Afterwards, set up the family room like a theater. Set up a concession stand with popcorn, candy, and soft drinks. Have one family member act as an usher by holding a flashlight and escorting each family member down the aisle to his or her seat. Have a good laugh together as you enjoy watching yourselves in the funniest comedy of the year!

DAFFY DINNER

Before dinner, prepare a small slip of paper for each family member to read and place it under their plate. On these slips of paper you have written down specific instructions for each person. During the meal, each family member will be required to carry out the instructions they have been given. For example, Dad's note might say: "Whenever Mom laughs, glare at her and eat something off the plate of someone next to you."

Instructions to other family members might be: "When Sarah picks up a knife, answer the telephone." "When Jimmy takes a drink, run around the table acting like a gorilla." "Every time someone takes a second helping, snort like a pig." "When someone puts their elbows on the table, yell 'Oh, no!'" "Whenever Tyler eats a piece of chicken, stand up and curtsey." "When someone says a family member's name, flip water on them from your glass." "When anyone says something mean, spank them."

During the meal each person closely watches the actions of other family members. At the end of the meal everyone guesses what he or she think the instructions were on each family member's slip of paper.

QUICK & EASY FUN!

You will be happy to know that there are many activities you can do with your family just on the spur of the moment and that take little preparation. Here are a few to try....

PENNY WALK

All you need for this activity are a few pennies. Split the family into teams, two or three members to each team. Begin on the sidewalk in front of your house. Flip a penny into the air and let it land on the ground. If it lands on heads, face right and begin walking down the sidewalk. If it lands on tails, face left and begin walking down the sidewalk. As you reach a corner or intersection, flip the coin again. Heads you turn to the right, tails you turn to the left.

Continue in this manner at each corner you come to. Each team must hike for at least one-half hour. Then, at the pre-determined time, each team tries to make their way back home, flipping their penny at each corner. See who gets back first! Be prepared to do some "creative" flipping of the coin in order to get you headed back towards home (or, in other words: cheat if you have to) or you may end up in Nova Scotia! Be certain to have some prizes waiting to present to winners and losers, for example: "Smarties" for the winners, "Air Heads" for the losers!

PARK FUN

Re-live your childhood with your children by spending the afternoon in the city park, climbing trees, playing on the playground equipment, eating peanut butter sandwiches and drinking chocolate milk.

If your park has a small stream or pond construct boats using a bar of Ivory soap, tying tree twigs together, or by using light-weight blocks of wood. Build dams and wade in the water together. Then spend some time sitting on a blanket telling your family some of your favorite childhood memories!

DRIVE-IN FUN

One of the most fun activities you can do during the summer months is to go to the drive-in! Wait for a great family movie and load up the lawn chairs, blankets, popcorn, soda pop-- oh, yes, and don't forget the children!

If you own a pickup truck, park it backwards and set up the lawn chairs in the back for everyone to sit on. If you don't own a truck, simply set up the chairs in front of the car, wrap up in blankets, enjoy your treats, and turn up the speakers! Together sit back and enjoy the movie, the fresh air, and the mosquitoes!

MIDNIGHT HIKE

After dark, arm everyone with a flashlight and take a hike to a favorite scenic spot with which you are familiar. Use the flashlights, of course, to find your way. Take a backpack filled with treats with you, which you can eat when you reach your destination. If you live in town and don't want to alarm the neighbors--or the POLICE--do this activity when on a camping trip!

FLY KITES

Kites are a very inexpensive investment for the amount of enjoyment they can bring. Purchase one for each member of the family, having each person assemble their own complete with a long tail. Go to a large field or park, and see who can get their kite up first and who can get theirs to go the highest.

After the kite flying have a kite cake. Make your cake in a 13" x 9" x 2" rectangular pan. When cooled, remove the cake from the pan and cut into the shape of a kite. Frost the cake and decorate using string licorice as the kite string and tail. Cut square cookies into triangles and place them on the kite tail to represent the knots that tie the tail rags together.

WATER BALLOON BASH

An easy and inexpensive way to spend the afternoon is having a water fight with the children! Let each child, if they are old enough to do it, fill their own balloons with water, placing these armaments in their own laundry basket. Additional weapons might include a plastic wading pool filled with water, buckets, and a garden hose. Divide into two teams-- Dad is Team #1, and the children are Team #2. Meanwhile you, Mom, can man the camera and dry the tears!

THE WILD WORLD OF SPORTS!

As soon as Spring has sprung take advantage of the nice weather and have a sports marathon! Start out by playing baseball at the local park. When our children were little we played with a plastic ball and bat. If you have small children, stretch a string across the living room of your house and play balloon volleyball.

Next, you may want to play flag football. For the flags, simply cut some 15" strips of fabric. Tuck two inches inside the pants at the waist, allowing the flags to hang down over the hips. Also, if available, go to the local pool and swim; or play soccer at the park. You may wish to even add a quick game of basketball to this gala event.

That evening, following a vigorous day of physical fun, have an all-American meal! Hot dogs, root beer in a can, a bag of potato chips, and an ice cream cone!

WINTER FROLIC

Dress everyone in warm clothes and get your snow shovels and brooms out for a morning of fun. Before your friends or neighbors are up and about, shovel their walks and driveways. Then it's time for snow fun and games!

You may want to start by building a snowman, making snow sculptures, and playing fox and geese at the park. Make a target and give every one ten tries to hit it with a snowball. Have an icicle hunt for the weirdest shape, the longest, the smallest, the fattest, etc.

Next, play miniature snow golf. Bury plastic or styrofoam cups down in the snow. Use a light, plastic golf ball and plastic club or putter and play a round or two. Following the festivities, head home for hot chocolate, Hostess snowballs, and a good feeling!

YARN HUNT

A fun and easy-to-prepare activity can be created right in your own backyard by simply using a ball of yarn. If your yard is fairly large, you can tie several balls of yarn together, end-to-end, for extra length. Tie one end of the yarn to an object near the back door of your house and then wrap the yarn around swings, trees and fences. Send the children outside together, instructing them to take turns at winding up the yarn on a stick or pencil as they go. At the end of their journey a special treat will be found!

As an alternative, if you have sufficient yarn and time permits, have a separate string of yarn for each child to follow. Make a game of it! The first one back into the house with the yarn all wound on the stick receives a special treat (but be certain to have some treat for *all* to enjoy!).

A MUD FEST!

Our family loves mud! Find or *make* a slick muddy area. We use our garden spot just before planting. Or, wait until mid-summer when the river or reservoir water gets low and the mud on the banks is nice and thick. Perhaps your area has a "mud bog" car racing contest at the county fair. Wait until the big event is over and then the next day go down and use the already prepared area!

Have everyone dress in their grubbies (cut-off blue jeans work well) and have a mud fight, play tug of war, and mud football! Be sure that every one is covered in mud from head to toe!

Following the frolic, load the kids in the back of a pickup truck, go home and wash down every one with the garden hose. Then serve Mud Pies!

Recipe for Mud Pies

1/3 cup cocoa

4 eggs

1-1/2 cups flour

2 tsp. vanilla

1 pkg. mini marshmallows

2 cubes margarine

2 cups sugar

Frosting: ½ cube margarine, 1-1/2 cup powdered sugar, 1/3 cup cocoa, 1/3 cup milk.

Combine the margarine, sugar, and cocoa. Add eggs and remaining ingredients except the marshmallows. Cook in a long rectangular pan or on a cookie sheet for thirty minutes at 375 degrees. Take from oven and allow to cool. Spread the package of marshmallows over the top and return to oven for about three minutes, allowing the marshmallows to swell. Remove again from the oven and cool for one-half hour. Then frost and place in the refrigerator.

Wild and Crazy Family Time

Everyone loves to have--or to go to--a PARTY! In fact, just adding the word "Party" to any activity increases the anticipation and adds excitement to the event! Here are a few major "memory-makers" which you can try as a family, or enjoy along with several other families you wish to invite. These party ideas take a bit of planning, but are still very easy to put together and will create loads of laughs and fun--and are well worth the effort!

WATER PARTY

One of the most memorable events you can plan for the summer months is a family water party. With a little preparation, your family can have hours of fun!

Here are some fun activities for your party:

Water Balloon Toss

Have each family member choose a partner and have the partners stand facing each other. One member of each pair is given a water balloon. Upon the command of "GO" each person with a water balloon must toss it to his or her partner. If anyone drops a balloon and it breaks, that team is out of the contest. If the balloon is successfully caught, both team members must take one step backwards and the water balloon is tossed again. Continue in this manner, tossing the water balloon back and forth, and after each successful catch increasing the distance between individuals. See which team can toss the balloon the furthest without breaking it!

Musical Squirt Guns

Have everyone sit in a circle on the grass. Turn on some Beach Boys music and begin passing a large super-soaker squirt gun (or, a small squirt gun will do) from one person to the next around the circle. When the music stops, the person holding the squirt gun gets to squirt the two people seated beside him. Then, start the music again and continue passing the squirt gun around the circle until the music stops. Continue in this manner until the music tape is over or until the squirt gun runs out of water. At the end of this game, the person who is the most soaked is rewarded with a treat of frozen water (Popsicle!).

Hose Hockey

Use two garden hoses--one connected to the water spigot in the back yard and the other hooked up to the spigot in the front yard. Make two lines by placing two pieces of rope on the lawn, parallel to each other and about thirty feet apart.

Place a large plastic ball on the ground half-way between the two lines. Divide into two teams. One member of each team takes one of the hoses and on the command of "GO" tries to push the ball across the opposite line by spraying the ball with water. Take turns while other teammates watch and cheer! Keep score--the team with the most points wins!

JELL-O Slurping Contest

Make up several packages of JELL-O following the instructions on the package except adding an extra one-fourth of the water called for, so that the JELL-O is somewhat less firm.

Fill paper cups with equal portions of the JELL-O and give one of these cups--and a straw--to each person. Using the straw, the first person to successfully slurp all the gelatin from his paper cup is the winner!

Water Volleyball

Set up a volleyball net in your yard or, if not readily available, simply tie a rope between the house and a tree. Fill in advance at least four or five dozen water balloons and place them near the playing area. Divide into two teams, with the teams positioned on opposite sides of the net, similar to regular volleyball. Each team member should have a partner with whom he or she shares a bath towel. The towel is stretched out between them, each person holding onto two of the corners.

Using the towel, each pair of players works as a team, serving, catching, and tossing the water balloon over the net. If the balloon is missed and breaks on the ground, the team that tossed it over the net gets the point and the next serve. It will take a few warm-up tosses and catches to become proficient at this, but family members will catch on quickly!

Sponge Ball Relay

Divide the family into two teams, forming each team into a straight line. Dunk two soft sponge balls (Nerf balls) into a bucket of water. The first person on each team holds the wet sponge ball against his neck using his chin. On the command of "GO" he passes the wet ball to the next person on his team who grasps it from him by using their chin and neck (no use of hands is permitted!). The ball is passed from one person to the next in this manner until it reaches the last person on the team who drops it in a bucket of water!

Water Baseball

For this game you will need the following equipment:

1 - 2 large rubber dish pans or tubs of water which are large enough to place your foot in
2 - Garden hose, connected to water spigot and ready for use
3 - Small plastic children's wading pool
4 - Plastic water slide or simply a long 3' wide strip of black plastic
5 - Two metal folding chairs
6 - Several laundry baskets filled with water balloons
7 - 3 large sponge balls (Nerf balls)
8 - Large plastic bat
9 - 1 bucket of water

Set up your playing field similar to a softball field. Place a bucket of water near the pitcher's mound, into which he will dip the sponge ball before each pitch. Place two dish pans of water at first base. The runner must have one foot in each in order to be "safe".

Use the two folding metal chairs as your second base. Place a water balloon on each chair. As a runner goes to second base they must sit on and pop each of these balloons before they can continue advancing around the bases.

Use a small plastic children's wading pool as third base--to be "safe" a runner must be sitting in the pool. Set up the plastic water slide between third base and home plate. Have a member of the team which is up to bat keep the slip-'n'-slide wet by using a garden hose. Use rules similar to softball except that each team only gets two outs instead of three each inning. Players must slide into home plate in order to score.

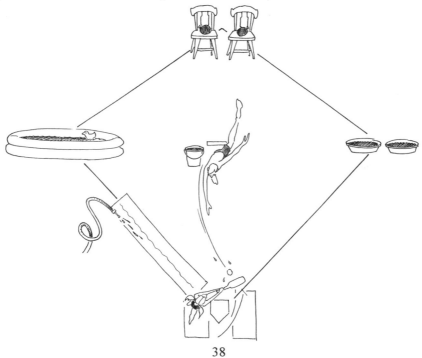

WINTER CAMP

Winter seems to last sooooo long and about February or March we often get the urge to go camping and enjoy nature. Although Scouts and Scoutmasters are dedicated enough (or crazy enough) to actually sleep out in the cold, most of us really don't think that suffering is much fun! For those who prefer being nice and warm, there is an alternative to camping in the snow. Simply have an indoor campout!

At least once a winter our family sets up our large family tent in the middle of the living room, replacing tent pegs with nails hammered through the carpet into the floor. (Or, if you have a free-standing tent, that's even better.) Unroll the sleeping bags and blow up air mattresses if you have them. For dinner, of course, we pull hot dogs out of our camp cooler, and roast them on the end of sticks in the fireplace! Add to this menu some potato salad, chips, Kool-Aid, and s'mores for dessert!

Using our special picnic tablecloth (to add a sense of realism to our adventure) we cover our coffee table, using it as a picnic table (or you can simply set out a blanket on the floor). For additional fun, play balloon volleyball in the family room, or set up the TV and VCR inside the tent and watch a nature video--such as The Wilderness Family, The Bear, or White Fang. Move furniture around to act as snow forts and enjoy a snowball fight using rolled-up socks as ammunition. If you are musically-inclined, sing a few campfire songs the children learned at camp, or tell scary stories as the fire in the fireplace slowly burns out! It's great fun and if your kids are like ours, they'd rather camp inside than out--the wimps!

FAMILY ROAD RALLY

If you are a two-car family, this is an activity you will definitely want to try! Divide the family into two teams--we usually have the boys against the girls. Give each team a paper sack, sufficient money to purchase or to do all of the items on the road rally list, a rag to dry the car after it is washed, and a pen or a pencil. Write up a list of approximately 15 items which each team must accomplish. Both teams get the same list, but one team will start with item #1 on the list while the other team begins with item #7 (so that you both aren't traveling to the same places at the same time).

All activities must be completed in the order in which they are listed. Two items on the list cannot be accomplished at the same place. Each stop will need a signature or some kind of proof that it was completed. All items on the list must be accomplished before a team can head for the pre-determined finish line. Following are some examples of the type of items that you might include on your road rally list:

1 - Find a bagger at a grocery store who has blonde hair and have them sign here:_____

2 - Thirsty? Buy a milk shake at a fast food restaurant and share it with everyone. Keep all of the straws as evidence.

3 - Can you find anyone walking their dog? Stop and ask the animal's name and get a signature from the owner here:_____

4 - Find an out-of-state car and write down the license number here:

_____

5 - Find a gumball machine and buy enough gum for each person to have six pieces. Have each person chew up their gum and then combine everyone's together to form a gum mountain as proof.

6 - Go to someone's home and borrow something from them. Place it in your bag.

7 - Go to a drive up window at a local fast food restaurant. Purchase one hamburger. Let everyone have a bite, but save one bite and drop it in your bag!

8 - Find a park with lots of playground equipment. Each team member must try out each piece of equipment. Someone at the park who saw you do this must sign here:

9 - Are they giving free samples at the grocery store today? Have each team member try one of the sample items, and keep one for the bag.

10 - Find a copy machine and make a copy of one team member's hand. Keep the copy!

11 - Go to a car wash and clean your car. Don't forget to dry it good! Evidence is the wet towel.

12 - Go to the gas station and put fifty-cents of gasoline in your car. Don't forget the receipt!

13 - Do you see a flower garden somewhere? Ask the owner if you can please pick one flower and place it in the bag!

14 - Go into a restaurant and ask if you can have a napkin which has their logo on it. Place napkin in the bag.

15 - Stop someone you know while driving down the road and ask them to let you wash their windshield at a nearby gas station. Keep the wet paper towel.

16 - Make a telephone call from a pay phone. Give the name of who they must call and the question they must ask this person. Write down their answer here:_____

(Arrange in advance for this person to give a specific answer to this question, which will act as proof that the team did make the phone call)

After finishing all of the above activities, the first team back to the starting point is the winner. However, they must report to the other team where they went to accomplish each item and display their proof. For awards, the winners might receive a "100 GRAND" candy bar, while the losers receive a Rocky Road candy bar or a Dum Dum sucker!

THE BATTLING RELAY

This is an activity that can be enjoyed by family members of all ages. Be sure to invite one or two other families to participate in this activity with you--the more the merrier! This party works best if held in a large gym or recreation hall or, during the summer months, this can be done outside in your backyard. Begin by dividing into two or three teams, making certain to evenly distribute little people and big people to make the contests as fair as possible. Then "let the games begin!" Here are a few possibilities:

Blind Man's Race

Lay two 12' pieces of rope on the floor about eight feet apart. Have players remove their shoes and stand bare foot on the rope. Blind fold two players (one from each team) and spin them around to make them dizzy. At the signal "GO" each player must feel his way along the rope with his feet. His feet must be on the rope at all times or he must go back to the beginning and start over again. When he reaches the end of the rope he must take off his blindfold, run back to the start and blindfold the next player on his team. Repeat this until each team member has a turn. The first team finished wins!

Balloon Bash

Give each person two balloons to blow up and tie off. Then hand them two pieces or yarn or string to tie the balloons to their ankles. At the command of "GO" each person tries to break the other team members' balloons by stomping on them. At the same time, of course, each person tries to protect his or her own balloons. Time this event for three or four minutes. The team who has the most surviving balloons wins!

Newspaper Race

Each person receives two sheets of newspaper. Line up in two (or three) teams. The first team member begins by setting one of his sheets of newspaper on the ground in front of him and then stepping on it. He then places his other sheet in front of him and steps on it. He then reaches back and picks up the first sheet and again places it in front of him, continuing to move forward in this manner. Once past the finish line the next member of his teams begins. This continues until all members of the team have made it across the finish line. The first team to accomplish this wins!

Nylon Race

Blindfold the first member of each team and have them put on gloves. Upon the command of "GO" they must put on a pair of panty hose over their shoes and pull them up to their waist. They must then take the panty hose off and give them--along with the blindfold and gloves--to their next teammate in line. Be certain to tell the contestants that you will be wearing these to church on Sunday so be careful not to cause any runs in them!

Ice Cream Bombs

One member of each team lies on the ground with a towel under his head while another team member stands on a chair next to him. The person on the chair holds a bowl of ice cream and a large spoon in his hands about waist high.

On "GO" each person standing on a chair attempts to drop a scoop of ice cream directly into his team member's mouth. Team members can take turns standing on the chair and dropping the ice cream. The team to get the most ice cream in their team member's mouth wins!

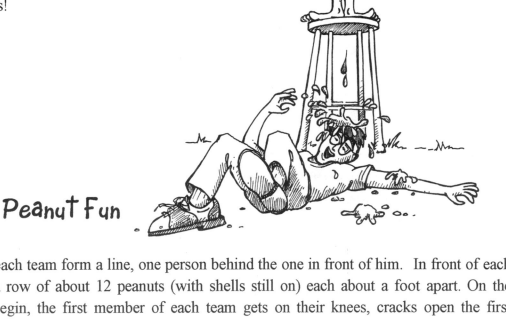

Peanut Fun

Have each team form a line, one person behind the one in front of him. In front of each team, set a row of about 12 peanuts (with shells still on) each about a foot apart. On the signal to begin, the first member of each team gets on their knees, cracks open the first peanut and eats it. Then they move up to the second peanut, crack it and eat it--and continue in this manner until they have broken open and eaten all twelve peanuts.

While this is taking place one of the judges is placing another line of peanuts on the floor nearby for the next player to crack and eat. When the first team member has the last peanut in their mouth the second team member begins. This continues until all team members have had a turn.

Tug-of-War

Give each person a string that is about six feet long and has a marshmallow tied about six inches from one end. The end of the string nearest to the marshmallow is tied to a chair and the other end is placed in a person's mouth. At the command of "GO" each person begins gathering the string in his mouth (no hands can be used to help) until they reach the marshmallow and begin chewing it up. The first team to have all marshmallows securely embraced by their jaws, wins!

Paper Sack Relay

Each team receives a large paper sack into which several wadded up newspapers have been placed. At the bottom of the sack is a wrapped piece of candy. The first person on each team is given a glove to place on their left hand. (Right hand for a left-handed person) Without emptying the sack of its newspaper, each player must reach into the bag, pull out a piece of candy, unwrap it by using only his gloved hand, and then pop it in his mouth. He then passes the sack and glove to the next person on his team who must repeat this feat. (Place another piece of candy into the bag as they are about ready to begin) The first team to finish wins!

Chubby Bunny

Give each person a large marshmallow. Then, one at a time, have each person place the marshmallow in his or her mouth and say "Chubby Bunny!" Give everyone a second marshmallow and repeat the process. Inform the players that the marshmallows must remain in their mouth and not be swallowed.

Have each person continue to place more and more marshmallows in their mouths and then say "Chubby Bunny!" People are eliminated from the competition when they can longer fit any more marshmallows in their mouth or are unable to repeat the phrase. The team that has been able to collectively place the most marshmallows in their mouths is the winner!

Balloon Sweep

The first player on each team is given a broom and a balloon. Using the broom they must sweep the balloon to a designated spot and then back again to the starting point. The broom is then passed to the next team member who repeats this feat.

Shaving Relay

Set up two chairs and next to each place a bottle of shaving cream, a towel, and a plastic knife. Each team member chooses a partner, one to be the "shaver" and the other to be the "shavee"! On "GO" the first pair on each team runs to the chair. One person sits down while the other spreads shaving cream over his or her "beard" and then shaves it off using the plastic knife (after each stroke, wipe the knife clean using the towel). Once the person has been cleanly shaven, the pair runs back to the starting line and the next pair runs to the chair to repeat this process. Continue in this manner until all the pairs on each team have had a turn.

Blind Monkeys

Once again have team members divide into pairs. The first set of partners on each team are both blindfolded. One of the pair is given ten peanuts that he holds in his hands in front of him. On "GO" the other person takes one peanut from his partner, cracks it open, and feeds it to his partner. He continues this process until he has taken all ten peanuts, shelled them, and fed them to his partner. The blindfolds are then removed and given to the next set of partners on the team. Repeat in this manner until each pair have had a chance to perform this feat!

As each relay or event is completed, give points to the winners, keep track of the score, and give prizes to the winners--and losers!

WACKY TACKY PARTY

Select several families to join you for an evening of fun. Write invitations on scraps of previously used or crinkled paper and mail them in used envelopes which were originally addressed to you (scratch out your name and address on the envelope and write their name and address above it). Ask all to come dressed in clothes with clashing colors, or which are worn inside out or placed on backwards.

Prepare your home for the arrival of your guests by hanging your pictures facing the wall and with furniture turned around or tipped upside down. As your guests arrive, show them your home movies--yuk! or, make them go through all your family picture albums with you!

Food Ideas

Eat on the floor under the dining room table. Or else, serve dinner throughout the evening, in the following order: dessert first, stale or very hard dinner rolls second, wilted lettuce dinner salad third, main dish of boiled wieners fourth, sour lemonade last.

Other food items to serve might include chips in the bag, pork and beans out of a can, peanut butter and jelly sandwiches (let the guests build their own), cans of warm pop, bruised bananas, etc. Or, simply serve TV dinners and Kool-Aid! Serve an upside down ice cream cone for dessert. To make this pour chocolate sundae syrup in a cupcake liner, add a scoop of ice cream, and place the cone upside down on top.

Non-Talent Show

For entertainment, have each person display a talent--in which they have absolutely **NO** talent! Assign, or let each person choose, two days in advance a talent to perform from a list that you have prepared. Examples might be: a ballet; baton twirling; magic tricks; Hawaiian dancing; tumbling and acrobatics; juggling oranges; clogging or tap dancing; a ventriloquist act; a lip sync; playing the drums, trumpet, harmonica, guitar, piano, etc.; opera singing; a dramatic poetry reading; and so forth.

Each person is given two days to prepare for his or her performance. They must have a costume and find their own background music. Fix a stage area and spend the evening being thoroughly entertained!

If time permits, finish the evening with a backwards obstacle course race: crawl backwards, run around the table backwards, have a backwards ball relay, and so forth!

BABY PARTY

A baby party sounds ridiculous, but kids think its a real "kick"! Actually, as adults, you can remain as "parents" (if you feel a little bit inhibited) during this party, which might help keep things under control!

In order to come to your party, everyone must come dressed as babies! Sheets or dish towels can be used as diapers. Bib overalls, shorts and knee socks, freckles, rosey cheeks, baseball caps worn backwards, pigtails, etc., are all in style! Allow your children to use their imaginations when it comes to attire.

Give each "baby" a candy pacifier (can be purchased at dime store) which has a string attached to it. This way they can hang it from their necks when not in use. Then begin your activities....

Play jump rope:

Use a large rope and take turns jumping and being the one turning the rope. Have the children jump to the rhymes they learned during first grade recess. For example: "Tom and Susie, sitting in a tree. K-I-S-S-I-N-G. First comes love, then comes marriage. Then comes Susie with a baby carriage!"

Finger paint:

Roll out butcher paper, newspaper ends, or freezer wrap on the dining room table or kitchen bar. Bring out finger paint that you purchased or do what our family enjoys doing-- use pudding. This way you can paint a little, eat a little, paint a little! Chocolate, banana cream, and red Danish Dessert are great colors!

Story time:

This is a real favorite. Have the children all sit in a circle while you or your husband read them wonderful stories. Dr. Suess books are some of the best--they are so corny!

Music time:

Put on some great classical or children's music. Give each child a five foot piece of crepe paper and have them dance with the crepe paper twirling around them, getting a real "feel" for the music!

Snack time:

Buy everyone a bottle of baby food. Be sure to use fruits--no veggies please! (My children think the apricot is the best tasting because it has tapioca in the ingredients!) As a part of snack time, make certain that the "babies" wear bibs (obtain these at McDonald's-- they have always been very willing to sell me some). Purchase the cheapest baby bottles and fill with Kool-Aid or baby juice if you find it to be less expensive. Also buy animal crackers or Teddy Grahams!

Tasting Contest:

Buy seven bottles of different types of baby food--veggies, meats, etc. Take the labels off the bottles and give the babies a big spoonful of each. As they taste some of these, you are certain to see some grotesque looks on their faces. Reassure them, however, that this food will not kill them but that it will help them appreciate just how hard it really is to be a baby--HA! Have them write down what it is they think they are tasting. The baby with the most correct answers receives a Gerber teething biscuit.

Rest time:

Have all family members get a blanket and pillow and a stuffed animal. Then put on quiet music to rest by.

Other activities could include a bawling contest, feeding relays, trike and wagon races or relays, etc.

One note of advice: To get your teenagers to enjoy and really "get into" this party, make sure that your curtains are closed and that you hold this party in the house behind locked doors! But get out the camera--you never know when you might want to blackmail them!

WINTER BEACH FUN

Have everyone put on their swimming suit and bring a towel--or wear sunglasses, shorts, thongs or sandals. Put on some Beach Boys music (can obtain from the library), set up some lawn chairs in the living room, put up a "Palm Beach" sign, and turn the thermostat up high so that it's nice and warm!

Improvise and set up a hot dog stand, where hot dogs and chips can be obtained. Prepare Kool-Aid or soft drinks, placing a slice of orange on the rim of the glass, and stabbing the orange slice with a miniature paper umbrella (which can be found at a party shop)! Purchase small, inexpensive gold fish bowls at your local discount store. Stir and pour blue JELL-O into them, dropping in a few gummy fish for good measure. Serve one bowl to be shared by every two people.

After eating, move back the lawn chairs and other furniture and play balloon volleyball. Do this by stretching a piece of string, yarn, or rope across the living room and attaching it to opposite walls about five feet off the ground. Divide into two teams and play using regular volleyball rules, using a balloon in place of a ball.

When tired of playing volleyball on the "beach," put on an old "Beach Party" video for all to enjoy--or spend some time dancing to, or singing along with, some Beach Boys music. Then try playing some of these games:

Lifesaver toss: Divide the family into couples. Stand a distance from each other and have everyone try to toss a candy lifesaver into his or her partner's mouth!

High dive: Give a person a pitcher of water. They must stand on a chair and pour the water into an empty tumbler that has been placed on the floor (or, for even more fun, have Dad lay down and place the empty tumbler on his forehead). The person pouring must not spill any water on the ground!

Swimming race: Fill a pie pan with water and place it on the floor. Place 4 or 5 lifesavers in the water and have the person get them out of the pan with their mouths and eat them--no using your hands!

Other activities might include a "beach ball blow-up" race (purchase balls through Oriental Trading Company for about $6.00 a dozen), a frisbee toss, and make sand castles out of play dough!

POOR MAN PARTY

Are you some of those poor folks like us who spend too much money at Christmas-time? If so, here's a perfect party for January (actually, it is the *only* party or activity we can *afford* to do during January!).

Write invitations to family members on old, crinkled paper. Prepare for this family activity by having everyone dress in their worst grubbies--pants with holes in them, paint-stained clothes, old beat-up and worn-out shoes, clothes which are too small, etc. Each person must give you ten cents to participate in this party. They cannot borrow the money from you but must search under couch cushions, inside of drawers, etc., to find the necessary coins.

Fix a special meal of stew without meat, or spaghetti with meatless sauce, JELL-O without fruit or whipped topping, and powdered milk. Let the children add some Nestle's Quick if they throw a fit! For dessert, bring in a garbage can. The can should have been previously prepared by inserting a clean plastic liner and filled with crumpled newspaper and candy. Have each person reach inside the can and dig through the garbage for their dessert— a half-eaten candy bar with the wrapper still on! (You previously ate the other half--YUM!).

Use old newspapers for a tablecloth and eat out of tin cans or pie pans and use plastic utensils. Place wilted flowers in a vase with no water. If it's winter, obtain these at the local floral shop--they are usually glad to get rid of them.

After dinner activities might include a Penny Walk around town (as described on pages 24-25), or rent a free video from the public library. Have a "bum fashion show" and vote on who looks the worst.

You may also want to play "Poor Man's Pool." To do this, use your kitchen table as a pool table. Use Scotch tape to attach paper cups to the table, two cups (or pockets) on each side and one cup at each end of the table--a total of six cups in all. The cups should be taped so that they hang on the sides of the table. The brim of each cup is level with the top of the table. Take ten sheets of aluminum foil and form them into ten "pool balls." Purchase two dowel sticks at your local hardware store, and use these as "cue sticks." Then spend an hour or so playing pool!

WINTER DRIVE-IN

One winter evening, tell the family you are going to the drive-in to see a movie the following night. To build anticipation for the coming event, hand each person a ticket that they can use for "FREE ADMISSION!" Make these up in advance by copying the suggested pattern shown on next page. The next evening, grab blankets and pillows, and pile everyone into the car. Drive around the block and then pull into your garage.

Beforehand, have the TV, VCR, and "snack bar" set up on a table or workbench in the garage. Hang a sign next to the snack bar indicating the costs to purchase soda pop, popcorn, candy, hot dogs, and dill pickles (one to five cents each--what a deal!). Turn off the car, and unroll the windows so you don't fog up. Let the younger children sit in the front while you and Dad sit in the back seat (no necking, please!) and have a great time eating fun snacks and watching a good movie!

PAJAMA PARTY

Early in the evening inform everyone that you are having a pajama party tonight. Have everyone get their pajamas on and grab their favorite stuffed animal. Serve a special breakfast meal for dinner: pancakes, eggs, sausage or bacon with hash browns and juice.

Make this a memorable evening by having a family pillow fight! If you are concerned about ruining your pillows, have a marshmallow fight instead. To do this divide into two teams and then divide your backyard in half (if you don't have a high fence and feel a little inhibited to be outside in your pajamas, use your garage for the battle instead). Lay a rope across the ground to make the dividing line. Give each team a bag of marshmallows to use as ammunition and let the war begin. You cannot cross the line and, similar to dodge ball, once you're hit you are out of the game until the next round begins.

Next, have a sleeping bag relay. Unroll two sleeping bags and place them on the ground. Divide into two teams and get ready to start the race. Use the sleeping bags like gunny sacks, hopping down to a pre-determined line and back again and then pass the bag to the next team member in line.

Then play "socks off." To do this have every one take off their shoes and get on their hands and knees on the living room floor. On "GO" each person tries to pull the socks off every one else in the family while keeping their own socks on. No kicking allowed. When you lose both of your socks you are out of the game and move off to the side to watch.

Play any other games your family enjoys. When finished carry your mattresses and bedding, or sleeping bags, into the family room and place them in front of the television set. Turn off the lights and enjoy one of your favorite movies, some yummy treats, and a family slumber party together!

CAMPOUT IN THE YARD

Set up your family tent in the backyard. Get out the sleeping bags, camp stove, and other equipment you normally take camping. Have a real campout dinner of hot dogs, pork and beans or whatever it is that you eat while camping. Don't forget the s'mores!

Following the cookout have an outdoor scavenger hunt. Give every family member a brown paper lunch sack and a list of items that they are to collect and place in the bag. For younger children these items might include:

3 flat rocks
4 leaves of different shapes
A pine cone
A flower
A worm or bug
A piece of garbage which someone has littered

This is a really fun activity after it has gotten dark. Another late evening activity is flashlight hide-and-go-seek. The person with the flashlight closes his eyes and counts to fifty while everyone else runs and hides. They must stay in their position until found by the person with the flashlight.

And don't forget the most important activity--ghost stories! Visit your local library for books!

HAWAIIAN LUAU

Part of the fun of any party is making the costumes to wear at the party! Begin by having everyone make their own grass skirts. For this, you will need to purchase a roll or two of brown wrapping paper, glue, and Velcro fasteners.

Each person should cut off two sheets of paper that will measure six inches longer than their waist measurement. Lay one sheet on top of the other and staple them together along the side that will be used for the waist. Make a waistband using a 3-1/2 inch wide paper strip. Fold the waistband over the stapled section of the skirt, so that half is on the outside and half on the inside of the skirt. Glue the waistband in place. Use scissors and cut the skirt in thin strips from the bottom up to just a few inches from the waistband. This will act as the grass in the grass skirt. Attach the Velcro fasteners in the front and back of the waistband.

You can either buy inexpensive leis (through Oriental Trading Company) or make your own from pastel colored crepe paper sheets and string. Cut out three flower petal shapes. Use these as patterns and make about a dozen of each. Thread the string through the center of each petal to form your lei.

Once the outfits are complete you are ready for the fun! To set the proper mood, turn on some Hawaiian music you checked out from the local library. Your Hawaiian feast might consist of fish and other seafood--or perhaps a roasted pig! Also include pineapple, kiwi fruit, and fresh bananas. If you're not into seafood or wild boars, have a Hawaiian pizza (covered with pineapple, of course). For a drink try Hawaiian Punch served in a punch bowl with a green crepe paper strip used to make a skirt around the bowl.

For activities, use your imagination to make up dances. Have a hoola hoop contest. Some possibilities for this might include : seeing who can roll a hoola hoop around an obstacle course in the fastest time; who can jump through the hoop the most times in a row while using it as a jump rope; who can keep the hoop rotating around their hips the longest while doing a hula dance, and so on. Also available at many libraries are Hawaiian videos that show scenery from the islands and Polynesian dancers.

BANANA PARTY

This is a great party to have when bananas go on sale at four pounds for a dollar, and it's an easy party to throw together!

Tell everyone that they must dress in yellow for this party. Then, as a family, use your creativity to prepare a Banana Meal. For instance, you may want to experiment in making a new banana drink, make banana bread or muffins, and have a banana split for dessert. For your main course, make a banana pizza. To do this simply thaw and roll out some Rodes dough on a pizza pan. Bake at 350 degrees for fifteen minutes. Take out of the oven and spread on peanut butter, honey, and sliced bananas!

Following dinner have banana contests: Who can eat a banana the fastest? Who can eat the most bananas in three minutes? Who can take the largest bite out of a banana? Who can peel a banana the fastest? Who can slice a banana into fifteen pieces the fastest?

You might also want to try bobbing for bananas, or have a banana cream pie eating contest. Play "steal the banana" (same rules as "steal the bacon"). Go on a banana scavenger hunt at the grocery store. To do this, split into two groups. Each group must list on a piece of paper all items in the store that contain bananas. The team with the longest list wins a package of banana pudding. The grand prize winner for the evening receives a "golden banana award"! (Prior to this activity spray paint this special banana with gold paint) Then, don't forget to tell banana stories at bedtime! (Does all this make you want to go "bananas"?)

Parties With a Purpose

EAGLE SCOUT "BASH"

Honor your son's advancement to the rank of Eagle Scout with a fun dinner. Set up a large tent (either your own family tent or one borrowed from the Scout troop) in the back yard. Or, if it's winter, set up a free-standing tent in the family room.

Set up tables and chairs inside the tent if the tent is large enough. If not, set the tables around the tent. If you live in the country, prepare a campfire nearby or use your barbecue grill. If doing it indoors, use your fireplace.

Roast hot dogs over the fire. Add to the menu other common campout food items such as chips, potato salad, pork & beans, and then roast s'mores for dessert.

Invite scoutmasters, fellow scouts, friends, grandparents and other relatives. After you've roasted your hot dogs, spend some time "roasting" your Eagle, allowing those in attendance to poke fun and tell humorous stories of dumb things your son has done on campouts, etc.

The Court of Honor does an excellent job of honoring the boys, but I think it gives extra incentive when you as a parent also honor them. On the night of the Court of Honor presentation itself, wrap up and present your son with a bag of Eagle brand potato chips or mixed nuts! Treats presented during earlier rank advancements might be a box of Brach's chocolate stars for the rank of Star, a box of Life cereal for achieving the rank of Life Scout, and give Hershey's "Hugs" and "Kisses" for 1st and 2nd Class. And, of course, a "Bigfoot Pizza" or a package of "Fruit by the Foot" would be quite appropriate for your new Tenderfoot.

BIRTHDAY PARTY IN A BOX

We as mothers spend our lives preparing our children to leave home and be on their own. And one day, it really happens--and they are gone! Our children go off to college, to trade tech, or into the armed services, and then perhaps get a job five states away. That means you can't be with them every year to celebrate their birthday. So, **SEND** them a party in the mail.

Purchase a few party hats, blowers, balloons, small birthday paper plates and cups, cake mix, a can of ready to spread frosting, and candles.

Because you can't mail yourself along, go to the store and purchase paper dolls to represent each member of your family (label each doll with the name of a family member).

Add a cassette tape with your family singing "Happy Birthday" and screaming and yelling! Wrap the box up with colorful birthday wrap and send it off!

"THANK YOU" PARTY

There's no better way to teach your children gratitude, than to have a big "Thank You" bash for those who have served your family during the past year! The end of the school year, when it's beginning to get nice out, is an ideal time to hold this backyard party each year.

Have your children make invitations for each guest you are inviting and would like to thank. Guests might include Scoutmasters, Sunday School teachers, school teachers, school bus drivers, piano teachers, and anyone else who has truly affected your family and its growth.

The children should help plan and prepare the buffet-type meal that you will be serving. Next to each food item, write down the name of the child who prepared it. Visit and enjoy the meal together and then, if your children are willing and able, let them provide entertainment by showing off some of their wonderful talents!

END OF SCHOOL CELEBRATION

One of the biggest events of the year to children is the last day of school! Without too much work being involved, you can celebrate this day in a BIG WAY by having a banquet and giving out graduation diplomas right in your own home!

Small cardboard hats with a tassel can be purchased at most party shops for about $1.25 each. You may want to purchase white for the girls and black for the boys. It will feel even more special if everyone dresses in their best clothes.

For each child decorate the outside of a small paper lunch bag with a school stamp or draw and color a picture of an apple or school bus on it. Any cute design will make the sack look special.

Buy the smallest bread pan available and bake a loaf of bread in it. If you don't generally mix and bake your own bread, Rhodes frozen bread dough is available at your grocer's and works great. Just let it thaw out and form it into small loaves. After baking, slice the bread and make mini-sandwiches using peanut butter and jam, or tuna, etc. Place the sandwiches in Handi-Wrap and place in the sack.

At a five and dime store, or wherever they have a large variety of candy, purchase some mini-soda pops (the kind that come in small wax bottles). Place these into your hand-decorated paper bags along with two small "mini" candy bars. Add to this a plastic banana (with powdered candy inside) and a few small carrot sticks wrapped in Handi-Wrap. Have all of these items previously placed in the lunch sacks, so that when the banquet begins it will be a surprise. If you don't have time to prepare all of this, simply serve alphabet soup!

Decorate the table with New Year's horns, blowers, confetti, and balloon clusters.

DIPLOMA

*Congratulations*_____
on this your Graduation Day

_____

May Happiness And Success Be Yours Always

Make a copy of a diploma, one copy for each child, and fill in the blanks with their name, grade in school, date, and your signature. Roll up each certificate and tie with a black ribbon. If you do not have access to the Graduation March music (Pomp & Circumstance), simply sing it (DAaa...DA DA DA...DAaa...DAaa...) yourself while they march towards you, and then hand them their diploma. If time permits and they are willing, have them each give a small speech!

BACK TO SCHOOL CELEBRATION

The decorations for this truly **sad day** are what make this party so fun. If it is not really a "blue" day for you and you actually are looking forward to the children going back to school...**FAKE IT!** The table should be decorated with black butcher paper (obtained at an office supply store) and sprinkled with alphabet cereal. Using chalk, write math equations (1 + 1 = 2) on the black paper to get them in the mood for the tough year ahead! Use black balloon clusters in the dining area.

Use cafeteria trays like they do at school. If you do not have access to these make your own by cutting out from cardboard boxes and placing aluminum foil on top (or use TV dinner trays). Serve the meal cafeteria style, where each child stands in line and picks up their silverware, napkin, and carton of milk. You will act as the cafeteria worker and serve them sloppy joes, placing a bun on their plate and spooning the meat on top of it.

Place two carrot sticks on their plate, and then don't forget the canned peas that they hate. Finish off the tray by serving them canned peaches or pears!

If available it is always fun to wear a white cook's apron. Inexpensive ones can be found in the craft departments of discount stores. Also, a white paper cook hat can be obtained at a paper or party shop!

After the meal have a bubble gum blowing contest. Follow this with a spitwad contest. Spit paper wads through cardboard tubes taken from the center of toilet paper rolls. Set up a target, such as a trash can, and see who is the best shot! Next, divide into teams and dissect a peach. Each team must carefully cut their peach open, remove the pit, and then sew the peach back together with a needle and thread. The team that has done the best job wins!

BRACES OFF BASH

Celebrate one of the biggest events of your child's life by having a party the day that he or she get their braces off. During an earlier visit to the orthodontist, ask if you can have a few wires, elastics, old brace brackets, etc. Using this hardware and other odds and ends, create a boutonniere or corsage to award the patient following dinner.

On your orthodontist's letterhead and envelope, write a letter congratulating your child and have all family members sign it. To your honored guest serve a special dinner of corn on the cob, caramel apples, taffy, nuts, and bubble gum--or any other food your child has had to suffer without for so long! Decorate your table with mouthwash, toothpaste, dental floss, and tooth brushes.

ADOPTION PARTY

This is a great party to have when your child brings home their fiancee to meet the family. It is an opportunity for them to get initiated into your family and to impress them with how wonderful your family is. It also provides a way for the new member to get to know the whole family better.

Begin by having a special family dinner. Here in Wyoming, we would serve a real cowboy meal. Everyone would wear a cowboy hat and a bandanna around their neck. Our desire would be to shock our newest family member by displaying what a "hick" family he or she would be joining! I would serve some bottled sarsaparilla (root beer), cowboy stew, campfire spuds, and finish off the meal with cow pies for dessert! Then, for after-dinner entertainment, we might rope a few chairs and do a little square dancing to show off our Wyoming heritage. Determine what is unique about the traditions of people living in your area, and base your activities around them.

Following the wild festivities, slow things down a little by showing a few slides, videos, or picture albums so that he or she can come to know your family members and traditions better. Next, turn the limelight on your new family member, allowing him to tell about his background. Then, finish the evening by presenting a special certificate of adoption into the family!

CERTIFICATE

OF

ADOPTION

Presented to _____

Signed _____

Date _____

"SPRING HAS SPRUNG" PARTY

It takes some real creativity each spring to get the family excited about yard work and gardening. Tell family members that you are going to have a "Spring has Sprung" Party and that to participate in it they must first get dressed in old or grubby clothes. Don't let on to what you are doing--but then "spring" it on them. Yes, it's work day!

To make this into a party you will need to use a little imagination. For example, you might divide the family into two teams. Give each team a large plastic bag and see who can fill it up the fastest with leaves and dead grass. See which team can prepare a garden spot the fastest or plant the straightest row. Decide what jobs need to be done and then find a way to make them fun!

Since every one will be dirty anyway, add a little fun by having a "Flour (flower?) War!" Make flour bombs by wrapping about one-third of a cup of white flour in clear plastic wrap. Tie off the end with string or yarn and then poke some holes in the plastic with a pin or needle. Give each person about six "bombs" and let the war begin!

Finish the party by bringing out a "dirt dessert" for each family member to enjoy. To make these, use small plastic planting trays or pots obtained from a greenhouse or nursery. Line the trays with chocolate pudding and drop in a few gummy worms. Then cover with a thick layer of mashed up Oreo cookies (mash with a rolling pin). Hand a small plastic shovel to each person with which to eat their "dirt." You can serve chips on the side and thank them for chipping in to help you!

Making Memories

Every member of a family should be made to feel special. Here are some ideas for helping your family members to feel good about themselves....

THE SPECIAL "RED PLATE"

There are special occasions in each family member's life for which they should receive special recognition. This is certainly true at birthday time, but could also include times when a child has a part in a play, has just completed a successful piano recital, has achieved good grades at school, etc.

Purchase a special plate (at our house we have a special red plate, although any color is fine, of course) and glass to be used at dinnertime by the family member being honored. For younger children, you may want to obtain a bright, shiny cardboard crown, which can be purchased at a local party shop. Any such article or activity which will help a child or parent feel honored and loved on such an occasion is well worth the investment in time or money!

ICE CREAM MOUNTAIN

Another way to show special recognition to a family member after a special occasion (such as a Boy Scout Court of Honor, dance recital, etc.) is to come home to an ice cream mountain.

Pull from your cupboard the largest serving or mixing bowl that you have. In the bottom of the bowl place a generous amount of crumbled graham cracker crumbs. Then fill the bowl right to the top with scoops of two or three of your favorite types of ice cream. Finish off your creation by squirting tons of whipped cream on top. Place the bowl in the middle of the dining room table, have all gather around it, and give everyone a spoon. Take a picture to remind you of this special occasion, and then **DIG IN!**

"MILE LONG" BANANA SPLIT

Here's a fun variation of the "ice cream mountain" just described. Instead of using a large round bowl to serve your ice cream in, go to a hardware or building supply store and purchase a section of plastic rain gutter approximately 3-5 feet long (depending upon the size of your table). Place banana slices along the bottom of the gutter. Over the bananas, place scoops of your favorite ice cream. Finish off by spreading your favorite flavored toppings over the ice cream. If you like, add chopped nuts, whipped cream, and cherries. Place your "mile long" banana split in the center of the table. Arm each family member with a spoon, and let the fun begin!

A "HIP HIP HOORAY" PARADE

When a member of the family has accomplished something **really BIG**, plan a family parade! Use your computer to make a banner (or use markers and butcher paper to do the same). On the banner write: "HOORAY for DAD! He got a PROMOTION!" or "HOORAY for SUSIE! She's the new VICE-PRESIDENT!" or whatever great event you are celebrating. It might be fun to have everyone dress in funny costumes, bang on pots and pans, blow kazoos, etc., as you march around the house!

WELCOME HOME BANNER

With a large or growing family it seems that someone is always away from home for awhile attending something--such as Girl Scout Camp, Boy Scout camp, business meetings, visiting relatives, sports camps, etc. If a person is away from home for more than just a day or two, be sure to create a large banner welcoming that person home and tape it to your front room window for everyone to see. When the person returns home, they will immediately see how much they are loved and how much they have been missed. It's a great way to build self-esteem in a child (or parent) and to strengthen feelings of family togetherness and love.

"MONSTER" MADNESS

There are few activities that young children enjoy more than being chased around the house, grabbed and tickled, by a mad monster named "Dad"! This is a sure way to develop feelings of closeness between a child and his or her father.

INDOOR SLEIGH RIDE

Another fun activity that brings a dad and his pre-schooler closer together uses merely a blanket and a little muscle. Begin by moving back the furniture in the living room. Set a blanket on the floor and have the child sit on it near the end. Have Dad grab the other end of the blanket and pull the child all over the room. Kids love it!

Afterwards, have the child lay down in the middle of the blanket. With Dad holding one end of the blanket and Mom the other, lift the blanket and child off the floor, swinging him back and forth while singing "Rock-a-Bye-Baby". As children grow older and are too heavy to lift in the blanket, simply have the child lay in the middle of the blanket. Mom and Dad stand across from each other, lifting one end of the blanket and then the other, causing the child to turn over and over on the blanket, first in one direction and then the other.

DATE WITH DAD

Choose a particular night during the week that is typically free of commitments. For example, each Monday night have one of the children take their turn choosing an activity to share with their father. During the summer this is usually an outdoor activity such as playing on the playground equipment at a local park, going miniature golfing, bike riding in the country, or roller skating on the sidewalks and school parking lots. During colder seasons it might be going to a movie, roller skating at a roller rink, playing basketball in a gym, eating and playing at McDonald's, or going to the library and reading stories while sitting on the poofy pillows in the children's section. You will find that children greatly look forward to their turn to be with Dad....

SURPRISE! IT'S A PAJAMA RIDE!

At the end of a long day, family members are tired. This can sometimes lead to bickering or fighting among the children. Or maybe even **you** are in a bad mood! At other times, life just seems pretty dull. Next time this happens to your family, surprise everyone by announcing that you're leaving on a **"Pajama Ride"** in ten minutes! After all are properly attired--even Dad--jump in the car and drive around town, stopping at a fast food restaurant drive through for ice cream cones.

FAMILY SLUMBER PARTY

Children love to go to slumber parties. Rather than send them off to their friend's house for fun, invite them to stay home for a slumber party of your own. Choose a room large enough to bed down the whole family. Throw down sleeping bags for all, or drag in a mattress or two if your aching body rebels at the thought of "roughing it" in such a manner. Everyone should be dressed in pajamas, put in a good video, and have lots of treats prepared. When the movie is over, share a family prayer, turn out the lights...and don't forget that the most important part of a slumber party is the pillow talk!

BEDTIME EXCHANGE

Everyone looks forward to the weekends! Add a little fun to the occasion by allowing your children to choose whom they will sleep with--and where--for the night. For example, little Johnny may want to sleep with Dad in sleeping bags on the family room floor, while Mom will go along with the fun as long as she gets to stay in her own bed!

Enjoying the Summer With Your Kids!

Summer is a special time of year. It's when the kids are home full-time...and you can teach them full-time! Every summer the children get a break from their rough schedules-- and so should you. So take the summer off and enjoy life a little!

Get organized by organizing the kids to help you! Spend the morning cleaning the house (everyone has a job or two to do), do the laundry, spend some time exercising, and what you didn't get accomplished put on your "to do" list, and then enjoy the rest of the day being together!

Before the summer begins, gather the children together for a special summer planning meeting. Decide what kind of "days" all of you would really enjoy. Assign one day of the week to be used for that particular activity. For example, each Monday might be "Work Day", Tuesday is "Activity Day", etc. Here are a few possibilities to get you thinking....

VIDEO DAY

Rent excellent movies from your local video store. This might be a really good time to introduce musicals to the family; and don't forget the "oldies"--the older, the better the movie. Pick out the movies together. Don't forget the popcorn. Get out the pillows and enjoy an afternoon of entertainment!

SWIMMING DAY

Hey, maybe this will give you the motivation to drop a few pounds, if you know that you will be seen in public wearing your swimming suit each week! Or, be like me and just drive to a neighboring town where nobody knows you and go swimming there. This is a great chance to teach your children how to swim, to do a little exercising yourself, or to just frolic with the kids in the pool!

WORK DAY

My favorite day! Here is your chance to teach your children to work, even though it's sometimes more work for you to keep them working than if you just did the work yourself! Oh, well. This is the day to mow the lawn, weed the garden, do the laundry, teach older children to mix bread, clean rooms, clean cupboards, iron, sew on buttons, mend, clean the oven, etc.

Don't forget, after you've worked all day, to have "chips" for a treat, because everyone "chipped" in to help you!

ACTIVITY DAY

This is a day for a fun family activity--although often it will have to be done without Dad. Decide on some fun activities that you want to do during the summer. For example: a visit to the zoo, miniature golfing, roller skating, bike riding, a trip to a museum, a picnic in the mountains, etc. Make a list of such activities, being certain to get everyone's input and then do them on activity day!

EDUCATION DAY

Because life often becomes so hectic and busy we don't always take the time to teach our children some of the basic "life skills" which we really want them to have! Here is your big chance. Some possibilities include:

1. Teach your girls to sew (and your boys to sew on a button)
2. Conduct a "good manners school", teaching basic table manners, how to properly answer a telephone, how to act when company is at your house, a few gratitude skills, and so forth.

3. Teach your children to change a tire or to change the oil in your car
4. Teach the children how to paint a fence
5. Teach them how to properly make a bed, hang up a shirt, fold towels, etc.
6. Read the book and teach the skills of "How to Win Friends and Influence People" by Norman Vincent Peale

The list can be endless. Take advantage of this great teaching opportunity!

SPORTS DAY

Although the children are taught to play a number of sports at school, summertime is a great time to polish a few basic skills and to learn a few rules and regulations. For example, if you have a child who enjoys volleyball, but has trouble serving the ball over the net, have them take an afternoon to develop their skills. This is a good time to expose the children to other sports that they may never have had a chance to play...such as bowling, golfing, roller skating, soccer, baseball, basketball, and so forth. Although you may not be the greatest athlete in the world yourself, your kids will believe you're a real "jock" when wearing your new K-Mart sweat suit and yelling out commands! Possibly your children have never seen this side of you before, and you will be amazed at the respect you gain as their new-found sports idol.

PARK DAY

As parents we sometimes think that we have to spend lots of money on our children in order to keep them happy or entertained. Actually, most younger children are perfectly happy to just go to a local park and frolic on the playground equipment found there. If you live in a larger community, add variety by going to a different park each week. Be sure to pack a fun picnic lunch and a blanket!

BAKE DAY

In case you haven't noticed, during the school year there doesn't seem to be enough time to learn basic homemaking skills like cooking. While this skill is essential for your girls to learn, your boys will also need basic cooking skills while at college, or for training their new wife to cook as well as you do!

Teach how to measure ingredients, follow a recipe, and to CLEAN AS THEY GO; how to use a mixer, blender, and waffle iron; and how to stir, bake, broil, boil, roast, and fry! Start with easy-to-make cookies, and as the summer progresses have them prepare an entire evening meal, having all items on the menu ready to serve at the same time. Towards the end of the summer assign each child one night during the week to prepare the meal. This will allow you to sit back, watch a little TV...but stay alert for the sound of the smoke alarm and have your fire extinguisher readily available!

FRIENDS DAY

If you are not careful, every day can become "Friends Day!" But your children see their friends everyday during the school year, so summer should be reserved for allowing your children to become "best friends" and enjoy each other. When your children are continually begging you to have one of their friends over, pacify them by simply smiling and saying, "Let's wait until Friends Day." It works!

As the date you have chosen for "Friends Day" draws near, each child in the family chooses a friend they would like to have over. The kids plan the menu for the evening meal, the activities, games, entertainment, and breakfast. Mom or Dad pick the friends up just after 12:00 noon--this will give your children nearly 24 hours with their friends. In our family we have six children...times that by two and you suddenly have twelve. This may seem like an awful lot to take on--but remember, it's only **one day** during the summer, rather than having to contend with additional children in your home every single day, as many mothers do. You may want to consider the option of doing this on a Saturday--this way Dad can share in the fun. Also, if things get too hectic, he can hold down the fort while you pick up a bag of chips at the grocery store, taking at least three hours to decide on the brand to purchase!

Other activities sometimes include an evening video (occasionally viewed in the tent), climbing a nearby mountain, swimming at a water park, river rafting, have a barbarian or fondue dinner, or other fun activities. The evening slumber party sometimes finds the girls in the backyard, curled up in sleeping bags inside a tent, while the boys sleep on the trampoline or on the family room floor.

LIBRARY AND READING DAY

Pick a series of books and read them together as a family this summer. Have everyone grab a blanket and pillow, and lay down in the family room as you read to them.

Individual reading is also very important to keep up with during the summer months. Reserve one day a week to make a trip to your public library. Help your children to select some good books, and then allow them time at home to spend reading silently to themselves. Personally, I think an award system is the best way to keep a child reading through the summer months. Some libraries have summer reading programs, but if yours doesn't, or you don't want to participate, make your own summer reading program. Here is an example of what ours looks like. I post this little schedule of awards on the refrigerator door. After a child finishes reading a book and presents an oral book report to you or the family, they receive their prize. This is just to give you an idea--adapt it to the ages of your children and financial situation:

After 1st book   - Ice cream cone
After 2nd book   - Package of water balloons
After 3rd book   - Ticket to public swimming pool
After 4th book   - Candy bar
After 5th book   - $1.00 bill
After 6th book   - Popcorn from convenience store (tastes better than mine)
After 7th book   - Movie ticket or video rental
After 8th book   - Buy a book (paperback)
After 9th book   - Make your own homemade ice cream "Blizzard" by blending
                    together a favorite candy bar and vanilla ice cream
After 10th book - Happy Meal at McDonald's
After 11th book - Miniature golf ticket

Have some fun with this day yourself! I love it--I read more in the summer than I do all the rest of the year combined!

Wedding anniversaries only roll around once a year, but the next time that yours shows up on the calendar try celebrating it as a family birthday party...since it does represent the birth of your family. Here are a few fun ideas you might try on this special occasion:

HONORING INDIVIDUAL FAMILY MEMBERS

A week prior to the big day obtain a roll of butcher paper from your grocery store meat department or purchase a newspaper end at the office of your local newspaper. Roll out the paper on a floor or table and, while each family member takes a turn lying on top of the paper, trace an outline of his or her body onto it. Honor a different member of the family each day of the week by hanging their picture on the wall where it can be observed by all. Monday might be Dad's day, Tuesday the baby's special day, etc. Ways to honor the individual during "their day" might include serving them breakfast in bed, not requiring them to do any work around the house that day, cooking their favorite meal, playing their favorite game, and so on.

ANNIVERSARY BIRTHDAY CAKE

It might be fun to make a special birthday cake on the actual day of your anniversary, lighting one candle for each member of the family. Blow out one candle at a time and talk about how the glow from the cake is not as bright when a candle is missing. Mention how that just like the candles each person adds a special glow to your home and family.

STUFF A CAR

A really fun way to tell someone you love them is to buy 10 or 12 packages of colored balloons (purchase at $1.00 store). Write small notes describing why you love them. Roll the notes up and place one inside each balloon. After inserting, blow up and tie the balloons. Some examples of what you might write on the notes are:

I love you for going to work each day to support our family!

I love you for always hanging up your clothes!

I love you for remembering my birthday!

I love you because you let me drive the nicer car while you drive the junker!

The bigger the balloons, the better (they will take up more space). Get the kids involved, and even though it feels like you're blowing your brains out--it's worth it!

Load the balloons into your (large) car and drive to your husband's work. Stuff the balloons into his (small) car. On the windshield place a note (to which a small straight pin is attached) which states: "Surprise! Here is a pin! Pop each balloon and inside you'll find the reasons why I love you so much! Happy Anniversary!" His co-workers should get a chuckle out of seeing his predicament.

GIFT GIVING AT ANNIVERSARY TIME

Just as an individual's birthday does not seem complete without gift giving, it should be no different for your **family's** birthday. Have each family member make or purchase and wrap a small gift ($2 limit).

Earlier in the day gather all of the gifts. Take one of the gifts and wrap it in paper again. Place a second gift on top of the first and wrap paper around both. Place a third gift on top of the two previous and cover all three with paper once again. Continue in this manner until all of the gifts are on top of each other sitting in a bundle.

After dinner have the family sit in a circle and pass the bundle of gifts around while music is playing. When the music stops, the person holding the bundle gets to tear off the outer layer of paper and unwrap the first gift. Continue in this manner until all family members have received a gift.

BREAK A PINATA

Another fun family gift is to fill a piñata full of small candy bars and hang it from a swing set or tree. Blindfold the children and let them take turns hitting it with a bat until it finally breaks open. Piñatas can be found at many large discount centers and party shops.

With the family activities now over, the two of you can slip out of the house for a quiet evening together....

Birthdays are always special...and with a little ingenuity on your part, they will live in the minds of your children forever. While you may want to provide special activities tailored to your child's interests, a must are those ongoing traditions which you provide for each child in the family at birthday time--traditions which will always be remembered and cherished. Here are a few examples for you to consider:

OUT TO LUNCH

A fun tradition is for you to join your birthday person for lunch for a special one-on-one time. If the child is in school you can simply meet him at the lunchroom during his noon hour, or take him to a local fast food restaurant and be back before the hour is up. It's special moments like this that make memories.

BIRTHDAY BOARD

Anticipation is half the fun and a birthday bulletin board is a simple way to make someone feel special. Cover a heavy piece of cardboard with birthday wrapping paper. On top of this display a number of small and large pictures of different times in the person's life. This stays up on the wall for the month.

BIRTHDAY BUTTON

For younger children start a tradition of having a "birthday button." Take two different colored sheets of cardstock--on one of these trace a circle using a small plate as a guide, and on the other sheet draw another circle using a glass. Cut the circles out and glue one on top of the other. On this cardstock button write "I'M 5 TODAY" (or whatever the child's age) and pin it to the child's shirt or blouse to let everyone know that today is their birthday! While your teenagers might not be too excited to wear their "Birthday Button" at school, make them one anyway, even if they just wear it around the house!

BIRTHDAY DINNER

Make certain that you allow the birthday boy or girl to choose their favorite food for the birthday meal. Be sure to use your best dishes. Following the meal, before the cake is presented, have family members take a turn telling what he or she loves most about them.

BREAKFAST IN BED

Buy an inexpensive lap tray at a discount store--they run about $3.99 to $5.99 depending upon how nice they are. While the birthday child is still asleep in bed, gather the family together, prepare the child's favorite cold cereal (or whatever you have chosen to serve him) and march into his room together singing happy birthday.

This is also a good time to open family gifts and to take pictures, while everyone is around the bed.

AUTOGRAPHED TABLECLOTHS

Make special birthday tablecloths for each member of the family using white sheets or just an inexpensive broadcloth fabric. Have the guests at the birthday party or family dinner autograph the tablecloth with their names and the date using bright colored pens or fabric paints. Use the same tablecloth each year adding new names or repeating old ones.

THE MONEY GRAB

Have Dad save all the coins that he takes out of his pocket each night in a gallon pickle jar. As a traditional gift from him, he allows the birthday child to reach into the jar with one hand. Whatever the child is able to grasp and to pull out of the jar he gets to keep.

BIRTHDAY CEREAL

If you do not regularly indulge your children in high-sugared and expensive cold cereals, like Sugar Pops, Froot Loops, S'mores Crunch, etc., a fun tradition is to let the birthday child pick his favorite box of cereal to eat the morning of his birthday. Make it a big deal to go to the grocery store and pick out of that long isle of cereals. Then, when it's not a special occasion and they are asking for that $4.25 box of cereal, you just say, "When it's your birthday you can pick any box that you like!" And don't limit this tradition just to the children...I always pick "Lucky Charms" on my birthday!

MOM'S TURN

You've worked hard to make sure that everyone has had a wonderful birthday. Now it's their turn to let you know that you're special too! **Prepare** your family to celebrate **your** big day! Many times Mom's birthday goes largely unnoticed and for some reason it just isn't that much fun to make your own birthday cake and plan a party for yourself!

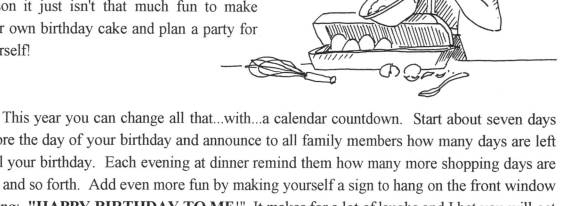

This year you can change all that...with...a calendar countdown. Start about seven days before the day of your birthday and announce to all family members how many days are left until your birthday. Each evening at dinner remind them how many more shopping days are left, and so forth. Add even more fun by making yourself a sign to hang on the front window stating: **"HAPPY BIRTHDAY TO ME**!" It makes for a lot of laughs and I bet you will get a far bigger celebration than you normally would!

BIRTHDAY BALLOONS

Decorate your home on birthdays to let everyone know you are having a special celebration for a family member! Balloon clusters are the least expensive and easiest way to decorate. To make one of these clusters, first blow up about 9 or 10 colored balloons. Take about a four-foot piece of curly ribbon and attach the balloons to the ribbon, tying them as close together as possible (about an inch apart).

Then take the two ends and tie them together to make a big cluster of balloons. Hang them throughout the house. Be sure to hang a cluster on the mailbox or on the front door to let everyone know that there is a birthday at your house.

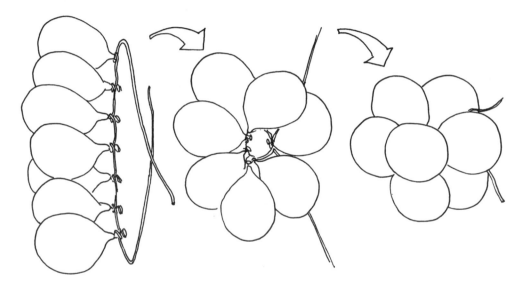

BIRTHDAY FAIRIES

A fun tradition is to have a "birthday fairy" come and decorate the child's room while he is sleeping so that when he wakes up first thing in the morning of his birthday he knows instantly that he is loved!

It's party time! Just a week after Christmas and it's time to **party hardy** once again! You're tired, right? Well, look at it this way...you have a month and a half off until Valentine's Day comes along...you can tough it out!

TURN THE CLOCK UP

If you have young children and are feeling "pooped," begin your family party early in the evening and set the clock forward so when the clock strikes midnight it's actually only nine o'clock! Then when the party's over you can go to bed early!

NEW YEAR'S EVE ACTIVITIES

There are many activities you can do as a family on New Year's Eve to make it feel like a New Year's party. For instance, go bowling and tell the family your are "rolling out" the old year and "rolling in" the new. Or, you can "skate out" the old year and "skate in" the new (roller or ice skate).

CRACKERS AND CHEESE TRAY

As a tradition, our family usually spends New Year's Eve at home. I take 3 or 4 cookie sheets or pizza trays and make a junk food fun dinner to eat while watching a really good movie. These food items include: four different kinds of our favorite snack crackers; diced pieces of cheese; sliced dill pickles; sliced ham rolled up and stuck with a toothpick; a bag of potato chips and dip; carrot and celery sticks with ranch dip; and for a drink, orange julius or pop. Later that evening we play card or board games (some favorites are Guesstures, Rook, Pit, and UNO). Then we take a night walk in the dark, and jump on the trampoline as a family for awhile. These activities keep us awake and help the time go by much faster!

REMEMBERING....

New Year's is a really great time to reminisce about days gone by. Home videos, slides, or picture albums make for a great evening. It seems like we never have enough time to do this-- what a perfect time to do it. Be sure to pop some popcorn and spend lots of time laughing!

BREAKFAST AT MIDNIGHT

Eat a light meal for dinner and serve pancakes, eggs, bacon and juice at midnight. Be sure to do the preliminary work on this meal early in the evening, before your energy is shot!

FORTUNE COOKIES

Buy a package of fortune cookies and divide them up between your family members. After midnight, **read into the future,** and have a good laugh!

NEW YEAR'S FIRE WORKS

Fireworks are really fun--especially for New Year's. Buy a few extra during the Fourth of July and store until the end of the year. At midnight, shoot them off. If you live in the city and can't use bottle rockets or other "highly dangerous" explosives, use sparklers and poppers. You may want to think of this as a science experiment--to see how sparklers react at 5 below zero!

LAST CHANCE PARTY

Invite several friends and their families over for New Year's Eve fun! Have everyone bring their leftovers from their refrigerator and pantry. Serve on your leftover holiday paper plates and cups from St. Patrick's Day, Valentine's, Christmas, etc. Use these to decorate your table--the funnier the mixture the better!

Take the whole group down to the local video store at about 8:30 p.m. and rent whatever is left over after everyone in town has rented a movie earlier. Old movies that no one ever rents are some of the greatest!

PARTY FAVORS

Don't forget to purchase blowers, honkers, hats, and confetti to throw at midnight.

Kids have so much fun with confetti (but if you use it, make sure that you're at somebody else's house--what a mess!).

The blowers, hats, etc. can be used year after year when you carefully store them, and they make the celebration twice as fun!

THE NEW YEAR'S TREE

If you haven't taken down your Christmas tree yet, take the Christmas decorations off the tree and do a fun memory balloon pop at midnight. To do this, have each family member write down four or five of their funniest memories about the family, each memory being written on a separate small piece of paper. Roll up each piece of paper which has a memory written on it, and place it inside a balloon. Examples could be: funny things someone said, an embarrassing moment for the family or family member, or a family activity that turned out to be a disaster. Then blow up all the balloons and decorate your tree with them.

At midnight each family member races to the tree and pops the balloons using their bare hands. Then sit down, read the notes and review the fun memories you had during the year!

PROGRESSIVE DINNER

If you celebrate New Year's Eve at home, try having a progressive dinner by serving some part of your meal every hour in a different room of your house. For example:

6:00 p.m. -- Appetizers, served in bathroom
7:00 p.m. -- Main dish, served in the kitchen
8:00 p.m. -- Vegetable or green salad, served in the living room
9:00 p.m. -- Soup, served in the bedroom
10:00 p.m. -- A drink (soda pop), served in the hallway
11:00 p.m. -- Bread or rolls, served in the basement or closet
12:00 midnight! -- A favorite dessert, served wherever the celebration is taking place!

THE HIDDEN ALARM

Hide an alarm clock that you have set to go off right at midnight. The person who finds it first gets a small prize that has been hidden with it!

"KISS" COUNTDOWN

Here's a way to give each child a special "kiss" or "hug" from Mom (or Grandma) every day for the fourteen days leading up to Valentine's Day.

Place a long sheet of Handi-Wrap on your kitchen counter. Down the center of the sheet place 14 Hershey's candy "kisses" or "hugs." Fold the Handi-Wrap over the candy and separate the individual pieces by tying a piece of ribbon between each. At one end place a giant Hershey's kiss or some other decoration, gift, or treat.

Hang this creation from your child's door or wall. (If you use a giant "Kiss" at the top, it can't be hung--so just place the large "Kiss" on the top of your refrigerator and let the small kisses hang down the side) Each day during February the child is allowed to use scissors to cut off and eat one "kiss," taken from the bottom. On Valentine's Day they will have reached the biggest "Kiss," which also can be supplemented with a "real" kiss and hug from Mom & Dad....

SETTING A HOLIDAY TABLE

The best way to make your holiday meal look so much more festive is to buy holiday paper plates and cups to set on your table. Make it a habit to hurry down to Wal-Mart or other discount store right after the holiday is over. You can purchase holiday paper items for as much as 50% off. Store these for next year in a holiday box. Use colored butcher paper on the table and balloon clusters in your dining room area--white paper is best for Valentine's Day, since you will want to cover the table with Red Hot candies (shaped like hearts). For candleholders, cut out the center of two red apples and insert a candle in each. There you go...with just a little effort it looks like a major production that you've been working on all day!

VALENTINE FOOD IDEAS

Here are a few ideas to help put a little more "love" into your Valentine's Day meals:

Heart-shaped JELL-O: Follow the recipe for JELL-O-jigglers as described on the package of JELL-O. Using a metal or plastic heart-shaped cookie cutter, cut out hearts and set on a leaf of lettuce.

Heart-shaped meat loaf: Make your usual meat loaf recipe and shape it into a heart on a large cookie sheet. After it is cooked and has cooled, use a squeeze-type bottle of ketchup to write "I LOVE YOU" on top.

Heart-shaped sandwiches: To make these you will need three different sizes of heart-shaped cookie cutters. Use the largest cookie cutter to cut out a heart from a slice of store bought bread--or if you make your own bread, add red food coloring to make a pink loaf. Use the middle-sized cutter to cut out heart-shaped slices of ham. Then use the smallest cutter to create a heart from sliced cheese. Place the cheese on the ham and the ham on the bread to make a really yummy open-faced Valentine sandwich!

Pink potato salad: Make potato salad as you normally would and then add red food coloring until you reach the desired color of pink. Place in a red bowl. (Inexpensive, colored plastic serving bowls can be purchased at paper goods stores or party shops) In another red bowl, place potato chips.

Heart-shaped bread sticks: Purchase breadstick dough in the biscuit and crescent roll department of your local grocery store. Lightly grease a cookie sheet. Form each breadstick into the shape of a heart and pop in the oven.

"LOVE POX"

Just as "chicken pox" is contagious, so is "love." As your children and sweetheart come to the table to partake of your **lovely** meal, hand each one a sheet of small, red round stickers which you have purchased at your local office supply store. They can stick these "love pox" on their own faces or on each other's. This will set the mood for one wild and crazy meal!

PIXIE WEEK

The week prior to Valentine's, have each family member draw the name of another family member. During that week, members of the family give secret service as "pixies" to the person they have drawn. These services might include treats under someone's pillow, making their bed while they are in the bathtub, polishing and shining shoes, ironing shirts, making special treats, etc. After dinner on Valentine's Day, have each family member try to guess who his or her secret pixie was. Then have everyone unveil their true identity!

EATING "TOGETHER"

Impress upon your family the need for closeness, togetherness, and working in harmony one with another. To do this, have family members sit in a circle around the dinner table, as usual. Using yarn or string, tie each person's wrists to the wrist of the individual sitting on each side of them (left wrist to the person on their left, right wrist to the person on their right). Then, let everyone dig in for a very loving and messy meal!

"HEART ATTACK" INVITATIONS

Invite another family to join your fun on this holiday by using this special invitation. Using construction paper, cut out 15 to 20 colored paper hearts--red, pink, and white. Sneak up to your "victim's" porch and tape all of these hearts onto their front door. On one heart in the middle you write: You have just been **"HEART ATTACKED"**! Leave information regarding the time and place of the meal and party you are inviting them to. Then ring their door bell...and RUN!!!

CONVERSATION HEART GAME

Here's a fun Valentine's game your family may want to try. Put two or three boxes of candy conversation hearts into a red bowl. Have everybody sit on the couch and take turns picking a small candy heart from the bowl. The person must then read the message on the heart and attempt to act it out for family members to guess. The first to guess correctly is the next to draw a candy heart and to act out the message.

MEAL IDEAS

With a large bottle of green food coloring you can have the time of your life!

Pick a main dish that is fairly light in color. Beef stroganoff is a good choice, and there are several other food items that can easily be dyed green. Add the dye to your stroganoff recipe and cook your noodles in green water. You can also add green coloring to your milk, as well as to the dough when making baking powder biscuits. Serve a green salad using lettuce, celery, broccoli, etc. Place some green coloring in your salad dressing--Ranch works nicely. Finally, serve green beans as a vegetable.

All together, that makes about 7 or 8 tones of green on the table. This meal looks very appetizing (?) and is especially good to have as leftovers, day after day, so be sure to make a lot!

If you really want to have some fun with this meal, dress totally in green. Dye your hair green using the 1 day hair color spray...and be sure to paint your finger nails green--that way you'll be green on the outside as well as dyed green (from your meal) on the inside!

Following dinner, serve dessert by having the family search for a "pot of gold." During the Halloween season buy a small black witch's pot (a great investment that can be used for two holidays!). Fill the pot with gold-foil-wrapped butterscotch candies and lead your family on a treasure hunt. As an alternative, in a leaner year, instead of giving a "pot" of gold, you may wish to have each person search for their own "Cup of Gold" (candy bar).

Begin by handing the children a written note that gives them a clue as to where in the house (or yard) they must go to find the next clue. Make the search long enough to be fun, but not so long that it becomes tiring. Six to eight clues are about right. Following are just a few examples of what might be written on these notes:

FOOL'S PARTY

Have a "Fool's Party" with your family--or invite another family over to share it with you. Write invitations backwards while looking in the mirror. Have everyone wear mixed-up clothes...stripes with plaids, shoes on the wrong feet, way-out hairdos, unmatched socks, etc. Greet your friends at the back door with a "Goodbye" having them walk in backwards. Have an indoor picnic, serving inside-out sandwiches with the bread in the middle. You can serve dessert first and have silly utensils wrapped in newspaper for each person to pick from.

SWITCH THE CLOCK

After the children have gone to bed, set the clocks forward approximately three hours. Then set your alarm for 6:00 a.m.--or whenever you normally get up. When the alarm goes off, wake everyone up, fix breakfast, and have them all shower, eat, and get completely ready for the day. When everyone is ready, just waiting for their ride to school, you might remind them that it's April Fool's Day and that they can now go back to bed because it's really 4:00 a.m. You will get some very interesting reactions to this announcement. But, if you happen to be a stay-at-home mom, the great thing is that you can take a nice nap to catch up on your sleep while they drag through school and work all day! HA!

STYROFOAM CAKE

At a craft store, buy a rectangular piece of Styrofoam that is approximately the size of your normal cake pan. Make your usual frosting--chocolate works best. Frost and decorate your "cake." Leave it out in plain view in the kitchen for all to admire and lust after! Pass around small serving plates and clean forks...now you're ready. Give Dad the knife and watch the fun begin!

DINNER IN THE MORNING--BREAKFAST AT NIGHT

The day before April Fool's, while family members are at school or away, prepare a taco dinner. Fry up the hamburger and add spices, cut up the tomatoes and lettuce, and shred the cheese. Cover these items with aluminum foil to hide the evidence and stick them in the back of the refrigerator. Actually, any evening meal recipe would work, but for some reason hamburger in the morning--especially spicy hamburger--just doesn't seem too appetizing. That's why tacos for breakfast just seem a natural for this holiday!

First thing in the morning, set the table, warm up the food, wake everyone up, and bring out the tacos and Kool-Aid! Yuck! Then don't forget dinner that evening...bring out the extra thick oatmeal....

CHANGING ROLES

When April Fool's Day lands on a Saturday, tell the children that to celebrate this special day, you are going to change "roles" with them. They act as parents, and you and Dad will act as the kids. Now, you might ask yourself, what should we do all day? Your job is to watch cartoons all morning and later go outside for a walk or bike ride. If you have teenagers you might want to take an hour-long bath, listen to the radio, talk on the telephone for two hours, and then watch television all evening. Your children will be really excited about their day. They get to fix three meals, do several batches of laundry, clean up the house, do the dishes, and other odd jobs. If you have teenagers, ask them to drive you some place--perhaps to a movie--and then ask them to wait outside and be prepared to drive you home afterwards.

BANANA HOT DOGS

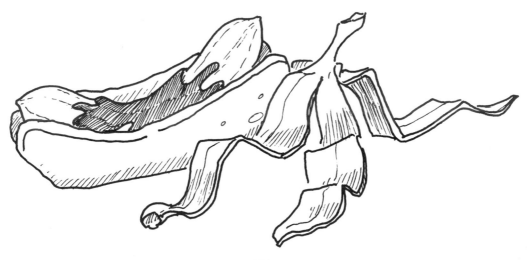

So, you send a sack lunch with your child to school and one to work with Dad. I'll bet you get tired of preparing those lunches. Well, here is one sack lunch you will truly enjoy preparing!

Take a hot dog bun and spread peanut butter and honey inside. Peel a banana and stick it inside the bun. Wrap in aluminum foil to hide what you've been up to. As embarrassed as they might be, if your family members are hungry enough they'll eat the concoction even if others are laughing!

Include in their lunch a batch of their favorite cookies...specially prepared substituting salt for sugar. Be sure to include three or four in their lunch. Don't forget to add some edible food too, so they don't starve. Perhaps about the time that school is dismissed you should hide out for awhile...perhaps at the mall!

DIRT DESSERT

Here's a real "dirty" trick that isn't too mean--but is fun. After Easter, buy on sale some small plastic sand pails with the plastic shovels. You will also need a few extra shovels. Fill the buckets up three-fourths full of ice cream. Using a rolling pin, crush Oreo cookies up in a large zip-loc bag. Pour a fairly thick layer of this "dirt" over the ice cream. Add two or three candy "gummy worms" and a plastic flower protruding out of the "dirt." Give two people one bucket to share, give each a shovel, and let them dig in!

DIPPED CHOCOLATES

Melt a bar of chocolate in a pan over the stove. Use several cotton balls to make some special chocolate dipped candies for the family. Have them prepared and waiting on the kitchen counter for your hungry children as they return from school. Watch the looks on their faces as the delicious chocolate melts in their mouths and their smiles of joy turn to looks of horror as they discover "fur-balls" on their tongues!

HANGING BREAKFAST ON A TREE

On April Fool's Day morning, as the children come to the table for breakfast, let them know that some "fool" hid their breakfast outside and they will have to go out to find it. On a tree, hanging from strings, they will find bananas, small individual boxes of sugared cereals, pop tarts, small individual bottles of orange juice and milk, and plastic spoons. String these items on the tree the evening before!

EASTER PICNIC

Decide what food items you would like to have for a fun picnic lunch. A few suggestions might be Hoagie sandwiches, potato chips, a raw vegetable tray, pop or juice, and brownies or chocolate chip cookies.

Wrap your food items in colored tissue paper or Easter cellophane wrap. So you should be wrapping about five packages. Hide the packages in the yard and have family members find them. Throw a blanket out on the lawn on which to enjoy this fun meal and--hopefully-- some nice spring weather!

EASTER BONNET CONTEST

Have your own family Easter bonnet contest. Give everyone 15 minutes to construct an Easter bonnet to be worn in your own Easter Bonnet Parade and during dinner. They can use anything in the house and can really use their imaginations for this activity.

If you don't mind a little extra work and want to make some really unique hats, go to your local newspaper office and obtain the end of a roll of unused newspaper (a "newspaper end"). Cut out about five large squares, all the same size, from which to fashion a hat. Lay down the first square on a worktable and cover with Elmer's glue--or make your own glue by mixing water and flour together. Lay a second square of paper on top of the first and add another layer of glue on top. Continue in this manner until all five sheets of paper have been glued together.

Find a bowl large enough to fit over your head and place it upside down on the table. Then place your glued paper--still fairly wet from the glue--on top of the bowl, and mold it around the bowl. (You can make other fun, really weird shaped hats by using objects other than bowls--like pitchers, oatmeal boxes, etc. to place the paper over) Let the paper dry and it will harden into the shape of the object it has been placed over.

Cut the brim of your new hat (bonnet) into a shape you prefer. Have each family member decorate their new bonnet with spray paint, crepe paper, bows, flowers, ribbon, or anything else they can find.

After going to all of this work, be sure to go over to a friend's house to show off your very fashionable creations! And don't forget to take lots of pictures!

EASTER HUNT IDEAS

Buy a sack of plastic colored eggs (the kind that opens in two). Within each egg place a clue which will help them find the next egg.

In this manner, send them on an Easter hunt, which covers much of the house and yard. The final egg will contain a clue, which sends them to a spot where they will find their Easter baskets, full of candy and ready to devour!

If you have both younger children and older children in your families who are involved in an Easter hunt, try this. Hide Easter candy throughout the whole house. Gather your children to one starting spot and then, upon the command "**GO!**" allow the little one's to start searching first. After several minutes then allow the older animals (ooops! I mean, "children") to start their mad scramble for the candy. This gives the younger children a head start and makes things fairer!

For an outdoor hunt, tie several balls of yarn together, end-to-end, for extra length. Tie one end of the yarn to an object near the back door of your house and then wrap the yarn around swings, trees and fences. If you have sufficient yarn and time permits, have a separate string of yarn for each child to follow and require them to wind up the yarn on a pencil or stick as they go. At the end of the string they will find some special Easter candy...or, if you have temporarily lost your sanity, perhaps some live baby rabbits or ducks!

EASTER CANDY

Following Easter, buy your candy for next year. Store it in a dry, dark place in your house—or in your freezer. You get twice as much for half the price. If you haven't any self-control, have your husband hide it from you!

EASTER VIDEO

Rent the movie "Jesus of Nazareth" from your local video store, and for several evenings prior to Easter watch it together as a family.

AN EASTER STROLL

After church, on Easter Sunday afternoon, go on a walk together as a family. During your walk, hand each child a paper sack. Instruct them to find and place the following items in it:

A small branch with leaves - one week before his death, people waved branches from palm trees as the Lord entered Jerusalem.

A small piece of wood - Jesus was crucified upon a wooden cross

A nail – the Savior was nailed to the cross

A thin, flexible branch or rope – the soldiers whipped Jesus

A thorny item - the crown the soldiers placed on his head was made of thorns.

A rock – an angel rolled back the large stone that had been placed at the tomb door.

Something that is dead - the Savior died for us on the cross.

Something that is alive - Christ returned to life and is living today.

LARGE EASTER BASKET

Obtain a large plastic laundry basket (purchase at a $1.00 store, since you will likely never get it back). Cover the outside of the basket using large sheets of colored crepe paper or tissue paper. Cut out a handle for your basket from a large sheet of poster board, attach it to the inside of the basket, and wrap it also with colored crepe paper. Add crepe paper bows or tie a large bow on top of the handle.

Fill the basket halfway up with crumpled newspapers and then add two packages of Easter grass to the top. Fill the basket with goodies or even put the makings of an Easter dinner inside: a ham, potatoes, rolls, and dessert. Deliver it to the doorstep of someone in need. Ring the doorbell and run. Include in the basket a big note: **"HAPPY EASTER!"**

THE GREATEST GIFT

Wrap a special gift for each person in the family. After hiding the gifts, hand each family member a piece of paper which has a clue on it which will help them find the hidden treasure. Clues might direct someone to look in the washing machine where they will find another clue directing them to look under the sofa, etc.

After everyone has found his or her gift, has returned to the living room and opened it, then ask: "What is it that gives value and worth to each one of these gifts?" (The fact that it took sacrifices and loves by the one giving the gift) Then tell how God has also given us a very special gift...much nicer than the one's we just received. He gave us the gift of His son, Jesus, and the resurrection.

THE EASTER BOX

Decorate a box with Easter paper. Place Easter-related items in it, such as: an Easter egg, toy bunny, small Easter basket, Easter bonnet or article of new Sunday clothing, Easter candy, Easter decoration, etc. Begin a discussion by stating, "Let's talk about what things make us think about Easter." Pull out one item at a time and ask, "Does this remind us of Easter? (Yes) "Is this why we celebrate Easter?" (No) The last item brought out should be a picture of Christ...the reason we celebrate Easter....

Father's Day is a great opportunity to place Dad in the "limelight" and for family members to express love and gratitude to him. Here are a few games and activities that could be used in a family program honoring him....

TWENTY QUESTIONS

Hand each family member a 5" x 7" file card (or piece of paper) and a pencil. Bring out a list of 20 questions that you have previously prepared. The questions should be about Dad, such as: What is Dad's favorite color? His favorite food? Most outstanding quality? His favorite hobby? Everyone must write down his or her answer on the card as it is asked. After all have written down their answers to the questions, start over by asking the questions again. This time each person must read aloud the answer they wrote down on the card. The last person reading aloud his answer, of course, is Dad. Continue on in this manner through all 20 questions and see which family member knows Dad the best.

THIS IS YOUR LIFE!

Have a **"This is Your Life"** presentation. Give each family member a card
with an outline of an important event in
Dad's life. Along with the card they could
be given a paper bag with props which go
along with the event. Each person can
choose other family members for his cast
to help him reenact the event for Dad.

THE FAMILY PUZZLE

Draw a picture of the entire family (if your art work is a bit weak, use stick figures). Cut
the picture into pieces and place them in an envelope, omitting the puzzle pieces of Dad.
Have the children put together the puzzle. They will immediately realize that someone very
important is missing from the family picture. Discuss how important Dad is to the family
and how unhappy the family would be without him. Then give the children the puzzle pieces
of Dad to complete the puzzle.

Other activities which can be used to honor Dad might include: the children singing his
favorite song, family members expressing what they like best about him, and a small gift or
coupon book of good deeds which each person will do for him!

4TH OF JULY

Here's a great opportunity to teach your children patriotism for their country. Take the time to celebrate the birthday of America in a BIG WAY! Use this holiday to teach love and reverence for freedom....

BACKYARD SLEEPOUT AND FIREWORKS

Celebrate Independence Day with a BANG! This is a great time for backyard fireworks--kids actually enjoy these more than they do the city fireworks display!

Following the fireworks, begin a fun family tradition of sleeping in the backyard all together under the stars. Be sure to have popcorn and homemade root beer for refreshments!

FLAG TREASURE HUNT

Hide several small flags in the ground around your home. Attach small notes to the flags upon which are written questions that the children must answer. Have them take turns finding a flag and answering the question. The reward for a correct answer is some red, white, and blue candy. (There are usually several types of such candy at the grocery stores during this time of year--for example, red, white & blue M&M's, etc.) Some of the questions might be:

> Who is our State governor?
> Who is the President of the United States?
> What is our State flower?
> What are taxes and why do we pay them?
> How many states are in the United States? Etc.

FAMILY DEVOTIONAL

As part of a special patriotic family devotional, present the family with a gift-wrapped map of the world. Have Dad be the special "guest speaker" telling about other countries and lands where people do not have the freedom which we enjoy--where they cannot attend the church of their choice, they suffer from disease, starvation, and lack of modern conveniences that we take for granted. A little research here can add so much! End with a special prayer of gratitude. As part of this family activity, you may want to watch Walt Disney's "Night Crossing" which recounts an East German family's attempt to escape from behind the "iron curtain," or the movie "Not Without My Daughter" (too intense for younger children).

FAMILY WATER FIGHT

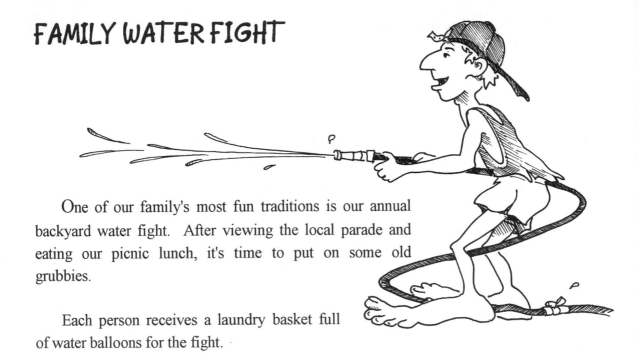

One of our family's most fun traditions is our annual backyard water fight. After viewing the local parade and eating our picnic lunch, it's time to put on some old grubbies.

Each person receives a laundry basket full of water balloons for the fight.

One bit of advice...do not buy regular water balloons--they are too small to fill and end up making a big mess. Instead buy a regular package of small balloons--they will work well. Then get out your plastic swimming pool and fill it up, placing a few large cups or small buckets in the water. If you have them, break out the "super soakers"--oh, and Mom, if you are going to participate, you had better grab the garden hose to protect yourself with--it's the greatest weapon of all! Divide up into teams--we usually have all the children against Dad...and I always volunteer for video camera duty because I hate to be hit by balloons! Smart, huh?!!

DRESS UP IN RED, WHITE, AND BLUE

Try this easy tradition for the Fourth of July. Simply have family members wear blue jeans and a red and white shirt all day! If you don't have such a shirt, wait and buy one on sale after the holiday, which you can use for next year. Often you can find one with an American flag or other patriotic logo on it. Or, you can purchase red, white, and blue bandannas for about $2 each that everyone can wear around their neck. These can be worn while attending the local parade or during other activities during the day.

PATRIOTIC MUSIC

Did you know that over 50% of all children do not know the song "America the Beautiful"? Take the time to teach them this, and other patriotic songs of America. Also, take time to teach your children to stand when the flag passes by in a parade or is brought into a room. If you don't have your own American flag, be certain to buy one and to display it in front of your house on the Fourth of July. You may even wish to have a tradition, like our family does, and have a short early-morning flag ceremony, at which you recite the pledge of allegiance, sing several patriotic songs together, and then retire to the kitchen for a breakfast of pancakes and eggs!

MEAL IDEAS

One of the easiest meals to prepare is a 4th of July picnic. Begin by decorating your table using a blue table cloth or blue paper. At your local dime store buy a package of small 1" American flags (12 to a package). Also purchase some red gumdrops. Insert the small flags into the gumdrops and place a flag at each table service. Then arrange a long line of flags down the center of your table. Be sure to use red, white, and blue balloon clusters, and holiday plates and cups.

Sandwiches -- Begin preparations for your meal by making red, white, and blue sandwiches. Make a tuna mix using 1 can of tuna fish, a package of cream cheese, and 1/4 to 1/2 cup of mayonnaise. Stir the ingredients together and then split the mixture into three bowls. Add red food coloring to one bowl, blue to another bowl, and leave the mixture in the last bowl white. Cut slices of bread into triangles and using your tuna mixture, place a red, a white, and a blue stripe on each. Or, using a whole piece of bread, decorate as a flag using red and white stripes and a dab of blue in the upper left-hand corner.

Layered JELL-O -- Obtain packages of blueberry gelatin and red gelatin at your local grocery store. Mix red gelatin as directed, place in a bowl, and let stand in the refrigerator until set. Then add a layer of blueberry gelatin on top, again allowing to set up in the refrigerator. Then add a small layer of whipped cream.

Potato Salad -- Using food coloring, this can also be made into three colors and displayed really cute in a colored bowl or plate!

An American Cake -- Using the recipe of your choice, make a white sheet cake. Decorate the cake using red, white, and blue icing...or use blueberry pie filling for the upper left-hand corner, sliced strawberries and Danish dessert for the red stripes, and whipped cream for the white stripes.

After setting the cake on the table, bring out several packages of birthday candles. Going around the table in turn, have each person in the family tell one thing they know about the United States. For example: the names of presidents of our country; sing a patriotic song; etc.

As each person tells one fact, they can place a candle on the cake. Try to add as many candles as possible. This really helps you see how much you know about our country. After you have used up all of the candles, light them, sing Happy Birthday to America, and blow them all out!

DINNER IN A PUMPKIN

Mealtime is always a great time to start a holiday celebration. Begin preparations for your special family Halloween dinner by cleaning out the inside of a fairly large-sized pumpkin and then use a black magic marker to draw a silly, smiling face on it.

Use this as a "serving dish," placing the previously prepared main course of your Halloween dinner inside.

(Note: Do not "cook" your dinner inside the pumpkin because it will take on the pumpkin's taste!) Some possible entrees include spaghetti, beef stroganoff, or stew.

Here are a few more ideas that can be used during your Halloween mealtimes:

** PUMPKIN BURGERS:

Cut out jack-o-lanterns from slices of cheese using a cookie cutter. Cook your normal hamburgers, place on a bun and place the cheese on top.

** PUMPKIN-CAKES:

Using food coloring, make orange pancakes for breakfast. Add a face by using chocolate chips.

** PUMPKIN PIZZA:

A quick and easy to make "pumpkin dinner" can be had by simply purchasing a round cheese pizza at your local grocery store. Make a face on the pizza using black olives which have been cut in half. Make the stem at the top using a green pepper. Pop in oven and then serve--everyone will be delighted!

** HALLOWEEN PUNCH:

Purchase a pair of inexpensive plastic gloves at your local hardware store. Fill one glove with water and place in freezer overnight. When ready for use, cut off plastic and place hand-shaped ice cube in punch bowl. Or, younger children really enjoy spiders in their punch. Do this by purchasing plastic spider rings, washing them, and placing them in ice cube trays. Pour water over the top and place in freezer. Drop ice cubes in a child's glass and fill with punch.

** GOBLIN SALAD:

Use cookie cutters shaped like pumpkins, witches, and ghosts to cut slices of cheese into Halloween figures. Place these figures on top of individual serving plates of green salad...or on top of a bowl of chili.

** TABLE DECORATIONS:

Decorate your table by covering with an orange table cloth (or you can buy orange-colored butcher paper at your local office supply and tape it to your table). Spread Halloween-colored candy corn all over the table. Eat by candlelight, or use a kerosene lantern...or set your table out in the backyard and eat outside in the dark, using only a candle or two.

TOMBSTONE ICE CREAM

Try this for dessert. Purchase a half-gallon of your family's favorite flavored ice cream. Completely unwrap the ice cream from its carton. Slice the ice cream into rectangular blocks, each block large enough to serve one person. Place the blocks of ice cream on a serving tray, one block for each member of the family. Crush a bag of Oreo cookies using a rolling pin. This will become your **"dirt."** Place this **"dirt"** over each block of ice cream, pressing gently into the ice cream by using your hands. Now you have made a "grave" for each family member. Using white poster board, cut out a small tombstone. On the tombstone, use black magic marker to write "R.I.P." (which means "Rest in Peace") and under this write one of your family member's names. Cut out and mark a tombstone for each family member. By gently pressing, attach one of these tombstones onto the end of each of the graves. Place the serving tray in the freezer until it's time for dessert, and then present each family member with his or her own personalized "grave."

JACK-O-LANTERN CARVING

Instead of hurrying to get the carving of the pumpkin quickly done, delight your children by taking the time to make your jack-o-lanterns look like true "works of art." Place a special pattern over your pumpkin and outline the pattern onto the pumpkin by using a straight pin to make tiny holes in it. Then use a small carving saw or knife to cut out the pattern by simply connecting the dots. Older children love the challenge and younger children enjoy helping with this project. You can obtain some truly fun patterns at your local department store, or they can be obtained from: Pumpkin Limited, P. O. Box 61456, Denver, CO 80206.

ROASTED PUMPKIN SEEDS

After carving your jack-o-lantern, be sure to save some of the seeds for roasting. Let the children help you gather the ingredients and follow these instructions:

2 cups pumpkin seeds
1 teaspoon Worcestershire sauce
3 tablespoons butter or margarine (melted)
1 teaspoon salt

Rinse pumpkin seeds until the pulp and strings are washed off. Boil seeds in salt water for 10 minutes. Dry seeds on paper towel. In medium bowl, combine all ingredients. Stir until seeds are coated with mixture. Spread on baking sheet. Bake 1 to 2 hours at 225 degrees F. Stir occasionally and watch for burning. Seeds should be crisp. Makes 2 cups.

HALLOWEEN DRESS UP

During the month of October, have fun with your family by having everyone put on their favorite Halloween costume. Instead of trick-or-treating, deliver special treats to your neighbors, extended family members, and friends.

TRICK-OR-TREAT GAME

Have a fun **family** Halloween party sometime during the month. Following "dinner in a pumpkin" and any other scary activities you may have planned, try playing this fun game. Have the family sit on the living room floor in a circle. Each family member takes a turn reaching into a Halloween bag (or plastic pumpkin if you have one) and drawing out a piece of paper on which has been written a note. On some notes are written, "You get a TREAT." If this is drawn, they are given a candy bar, cookie, or other treat that has been prepared. On other slips of paper are written the descriptions of "TRICKS" which the person drawing it must perform.

Place equal numbers of "TRICKS" or "TREATS" in the bag. You may wish to increase the action by having family members race each other in certain events. This gives more people a chance to participate in the fun. Following are a sample of some "TRICKS" you may wish to see family members perform:

1 - Eat a hanging donut (hang donut from ceiling so person will have to stand on toes to reach it with their mouth--they must eat without using hands)

2 - Squirt out a candle (light candle in jack-o-lantern, move person back 3 steps from candle, blindfold, spin them around; they must then extinguish the candle using squirt gun)

3 - Move the cotton balls (put cotton balls in bowl, blindfold & use spoon to get them all into another bowl)

4 - Recite a favorite poem...dramatically (Mary had a Little Lamb, or Twinkle, Twinkle Little Star)

5 - Blind elephants (blindfold two people--one shells and feeds peanuts to partner)

6 - Eat a pie without using hands (put chocolate pie filling in pie pan and place whipped cream on top)

7 - Do a witch dance (put on a witch hat, hold a broom, and dance to Halloween music)

8 - Shave someone's legs (use butter knife & shaving cream, wipe knife on towel)

9 - Put 5 pieces of bubble gum in your mouth, chew & blow a large bubble

10 - Put on 20 shirts, one over the top of the other

11 - Walk across room with pillow between knees, coin in one eye & plate on head

12 - Drink a baby bottled filled with Kool-Aid

13 - Everyone gets to squirt you with squirt gun 4 times

14 - Walk across room barefoot with marbles between your toes

15 - Have others wrap you up like a mummy using toilet paper

16 - Eat a "Big Hunk" candy bar within 5 minutes

17 - Choose someone to "fix" your hair (use spray can of washable hair dye, curling iron, etc.)

18 - See if you can put twelve marshmallows in your mouth at one time

19 - Suck pumpkin seeds with a straw and move the seeds from one bowl to another (race with another family member)

20 - Must take a walk outside in the dark...alone

21 - "Bob" for baby pumpkins in a witch kettle (use small pumpkin gourds)

22 - Choose a partner for yourself and then choose two other individuals who will act as partners that you will be competing against. See who can empty a can of whipped cream into their partner's mouth the fastest

23 - Choose someone to compete against and see who can eat a Popsicle the fastest

SCARY OUTDOOR FUN

Blindfold your children (or anyone else coming to your party) and lead them out to the middle of a field. Leave them alone there while you scamper over to the table you have set up in some trees a fair distance away. Have a lantern or candle lit on the table and eventually your guests will find their way to you. Have a ghost welcome them as they arrive and have a monster seat them and serve them dinner.

SPOOK ALLEY FUN

All children love a "spook alley." They love to go through one...and love even more to create and to be a participant in one. The size and layout of your house and yard, your own "energy level," and the availability of resources will largely determine how extravagant you might want to get with this little project. The children may wish to build a spook-alley just to scare Dad--or they may wish to invite some of their friends to go through. After sending their guests through, however, let the guests take a turn being the "spooks" while the children take a turn going through their own creation. Here are a few ideas you can suggest your children use in making their terrible "den of horrors":

** Have a monster act as a guide through spook alley. They can use a flashlight but hold hand over the beam to largely dim the light. Then take hand off and shine directly onto the faces of scary monsters when they jump out.

** For the best affect, be sure to put on scary music. Pre-recorded cassette tapes can be purchased at many retail outlets.

** A "Slip 'n Slide" can be made to go down stairs by using a mattress.

** Flip water on those journeying through the spook alley by using a paintbrush.

** Prepare a bucket of icy salt water. Dip gloved hand into it and place on the faces of those passing by.

** Use a spray mist bottle.

** Use large cardboard boxes (obtain at appliance stores) for people to crawl through. Cut holes in sides for arms to protrude through.

** Make a homemade coffin from wood or cardboard box. Place on top of table. The guide encourages people to go up close and see the vampire lying in it. While they are anxiously waiting for the vampire to come alive and grab them, a hand reaches out from under the table and begins grabbing their ankles.

** Squirt shaving cream on. Easy clean up.

** Someone can dress as a witch, stirring a pot with steam running off it (use dry ice in water for this affect). The witch can then take people to a table with various items to feel.

Eyeball = peeled grapes. Teeth = dried corn. Blood veins = cooked spaghetti died red. Ears = dried prunes. Liver = bowl of JELL-O. Thumb = cut-off hot dog. Hand = plastic glove filled with sand.

THE PARTS OF "SPOOKY LUKE"

Dim the lights, or light a candle, and have the children sit in a circle and close their eyes. Repeat the story below while passing the object suggested around the circle.

"Spooky Luke passed away...but parts of him are with us here today. We know that Luke will never again eat, for here are some pieces of his teeth!" (pieces of chalk)

"I hope this won't cause you too much fear, but this, it seems, is a part of his ear." (dried prunes or apricot)

"I hope you believe me, I would not lie, but it seems to me this must be his eye." (peeled grape)

"I wonder, I wonder, do you suppose, that this was once Luke's long sleek nose?" (piece of hot dog)

"You may not wish to stay and linger, after you feel his little finger." (large pickle or carrot)

"I hope this won't give you too great a scare, because this was once Luke's long black hair!" (cooked spaghetti)

"To you this may sound somewhat grim, but this was once inside of him!" (pieces of JELL-O)

CAMP FIRE "FREAK OUT"

Try this for Halloween fun. Build a bon fire outside and set up logs or chairs around the fire. Roast hot dogs ("Halloweenies") over the fire and have chili dogs, chips, and carrot sticks. For dessert, roast marshmallows and, if you like, add chocolate bars and graham crackers to make "s'mores". Then tell scary ghost stories around the fire. Your local library has many excellent books that you can use to find a few good stories to "shock" your family.

OUTDOOR "SPOOK ALLEY"

A fun and easy-to-make spook alley can be created right in your own backyard by simply using black yarn. If your yard is fairly large, you can tie several balls of yarn together, end-to-end, for extra length. Tie one end of the yarn to an object near the back door of your house and then wrap the yarn around swings, trees and fences.

Put on scary music and send the children outside, one at a time, clinging to and following the yarn. Be sure to have a few scary creatures jump out along their path for an extra thrill!

If you have sufficient yarn and time permits, have a separate string of yarn for each child to follow and require them to wind up the yarn on a pencil or stick as they go. The first one back into the house with the yarn all wound on the stick receives a special treat.

PRE-SCHOOL HALLOWEEN FUN

** Go for a fun witch walk. Grab a broom for everyone and ride the broom sticks like witches.

** Goblin hunt: Send young children on a spooky search to find missing pieces of a witch or goblin. Pretzel sticks = bones; Ketchup = blood; Peeled grapes = eyes; Yarn = hair; Wet noodles = intestines; Cauliflower = brains; etc.

** Stick a Wart on a Witch: On a poster board draw the face of a witch. Blind fold little guests, turn them around and see who comes the closest to putting the wart on the witch.

** Witches' Relay: Divide into two teams and form into lines. First person in each line is given a broom and a pair of rolled socks. Each player in turn sweeps the socks past a designated point and back again.

THREE FAMILY HALLOWEEN PARTY

Often, Halloween parties can be made even more fun for your family if you invite some guests--the old adage "the more the merrier" being oh, so true. Make assignments and divide responsibilities. One family provides the games, one family the spook alley, and one family provides dinner or treats. Then sit back and let the good times roll....

HALLOWEEN MOVIES

Share a Halloween "fright" together as a family one evening by enjoying a scary movie together. Here are some possibilities according to the age of your children:

Pre-Schoolers: Legend of Sleepy Hollow
                   Scooby Doo and the Werewolf

Grade School: The Ghost and Mr. Chicken
                      Blackbeard's Ghost
                      Child of Glass
                      The Private Eyes

Middle School: Wait Until Dark
                      Fall of the House of Usher
                      Watcher in the Woods
                      The Haunting

A MESSAGE FROM A MONSTER!

Here's a fun idea to try while you are watching a video. Ask a friend to call you on the telephone, near the end of the movie, at a pre-arranged designated time. Tell your children that you and Dad have to leave for a little while but that you will be back soon. Figure in advance when you expect the movie to be over. Shortly after its completion ring the front door bell. As the children come to the door to answer it they will see a sign on the door you have placed there which points to a cassette player on the floor and tells them to "please listen to the recorded message and follow directions carefully!" The tape contains a message from a very scary sounding man (actually, Dad) which might say something like this:

"I hope you have enjoyed the movie...(heavy breathing and moaning)...now, please come join me--for there is something I want you to see...don't be afraid...go to the back yard and go towards the candlelight...go towards the candlelight...go towards the candlelight." (use a Vincent Price type voice, and if you have a second tape player have scary music playing in the background while you are recording)

Meanwhile, in a remote corner of the backyard, have a table set with a candle or kerosene lantern burning. Dress in a large coat with scary mask and serve your children dinner in a pumpkin or graveyard dessert (as earlier described).

Thanksgiving

THE TURKEY FAIRY

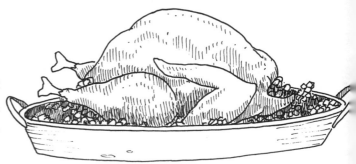

During the month of November, not only purchase a turkey for your own family, but buy an extra one that you can drop off to a needy family.

If you can afford it, you may wish to buy one for each child to give away. Let them choose the family that they wish to be a "fairy" to. Include a note: "From the Turkey Fairy!" Drop off on the doorstep after dark, ring the doorbell and run!

GIVING "THANKS"

As a mother, Thanksgiving is a special time to teach your children to be grateful. What better time is there to not only count one's blessings, but to give "thanks" to others who have

154

given service to your family. This can be done by simply making small treats or "mini" pies (since, after all, pies are a Thanksgiving tradition!) and taking them around to school teachers, church teachers, Scout leaders, piano teachers, etc. Drop off the pie at their house along with a thank you note expressing your appreciation; or place the note on their doorknob stating: "We're thankful to you for....," place the pie on the porch, ring the doorbell and run!

SERVICE TO THE HOMELESS

By contacting the local Salvation Army or other homeless shelter in your area, your family can volunteer to help serve the Thanksgiving meal to needy or homeless people. Because so many people are with their own extended families on this holiday, these groups can always use help. This is one of the greatest lessons you can teach your children in being thankful for the blessings that **your** family has! You will come away from this experience with a really great feeling....

MOTEL GET-A-WAY

For some who live far away from extended family and can't be home to enjoy the festivities with them, this holiday can sometimes bring on a feeling of loneliness or boredom. A fun activity to "beat the blues" is to take the whole family to a fun motel, where you can watch TV, swim, and fix turkey cooking bags which are cooked over a camp stove and served over sliced white bread! If you do this every year, it becomes a fun tradition to look forward to!

Christmas

CHRISTMAS EVE HOT CHOCOLATE

On Christmas Eve, just before bed, be sure to serve hot chocolate with miniature marshmallows floating on top. Then, years later, when your children are away from home at the holidays, you can send an envelope of hot chocolate with a small plastic bag of marshmallows as a reminder of home and the holidays....

RHYMING GAME

This is one of our family's favorite Christmas games. Give each person a pencil and piece of paper, or divide into groups of two or three people working together. Place articles around house in pairs which rhyme which each individual or group must guess and then write down (most of these items can be purchased in the "trinket" or novelty Christmas section of your local department store). Use a time limit (perhaps 30 minutes). See who finds the most.

Examples:

1. Ball in hall (Suspend round Christmas ornament from hallway ceiling)
2. Bill on sill (Place a dollar bill on a window sill)
3. Cone on phone (Pine cone on telephone)
4. Cutter on butter (Cookie cutter on a stick of butter or margarine)
5. Flock on clock.
6. Bow in snow (Christmas bow laying on batting or cotton)
7. Dime on chime (a dime taped onto doorbell chime)
8. Elf on shelf
9. Deer on mirror (tape miniature toy deer on mirror)
10. Sled on bed
11. Frog on log (miniature toy frog on fireplace log)
12. Pickle on sickle (Use ice sickles used on Christmas trees)
13. Lights on tights (Christmas lights on child's tights)
14. Limb on brim (small tree limb on brim of a hat)

15. Holly on dolly (Christmas holly on a doll)
16. Bear on chair (Use teddy bear, not live bear!)
17. Bell on shell (Christmas bell on sea shell or shell of egg)
18. Star on jar (Christmas star on cookie jar)
19. Cap on tap (Bottle cap on kitchen sink tap)
20. Spoon on tune (Place a spoon on top of your piano)
21. Note on coat (Note to Santa on top of a coat)
22. Rock on sock (Rock on Christmas stocking)
23. Key on tree (Hang a key on Christmas tree)
24. Spice on rice (Container of cinnamon on a box of rice)
25. Gift on sift (Wrapped package on top of flour sifter
26. Man on can (Snowman on a can of something)
27. Ring on string (Canning ring hung by string from a doorknob)
28. Nick on pick (St. Nick sitting on a toothpick)
29. Handle on candle (Screw driver handle on candle)
30. Fruit on boot (Apple on snow boot)
31. Vase on case (Flower vase on bookcase)
32. Teeth on wreath
33. Doves on gloves
34. Tag on bag (Christmas gift tag...TO: _____...on a paper bag)

PRIVILEGE CALENDAR

Purchase or make an advent calendar. (This can be as simple as taking a long piece of ribbon and tying your rolled up "privilege" notes to it.) Each day, beginning on December 1st, one of your children is allowed to draw a note from the calendar. A different child draws a privilege note each day. Be sure that you know in advance what privileges are coming up during the next few days so that you are prepared for them. Also, if you've had a particularly rough day, you may want to switch some of the notes around--when the kids aren't looking--so as to postpone some more involved activities for a later day!

Here are some ideas for your privilege calendar countdown....

1. You get a special back rub from Dad
2. You can have a box of special Christmas cereal
3. You get to go for a walk with Dad
4. You get to stay up an extra hour tonight
5. You get an ice cream sundae
6. You get 50 cents to spend as you like
7. You get to pick a Christmas video
8. You get to sleep with anyone in the family
9. You get to have a date with Mom or Dad
10. You don't have to do any work today
11. You get a pack of gum to give away to all your friends
12. You can go Christmas shopping today
13. You can pick whatever you'd like for dinner

14. You can make gingerbread boys or Christmas cookies
15. You can have a friend sleep over
16. You get to sleep under the Christmas tree
17. You can pick your favorite game & the family will play it with you
18. You get breakfast in bed
19. You get to go see Christmas lights--& have donuts and hot chocolate too!
20. You get to make "s'mores" over the fireplace (or stove)
21. You get to eat breakfast at McDonald's with Dad
22. You get to pick two of your favorite candy bars
23. You get to go visit Santa Claus today
24. You get to open one small gift under the tree tonight
25. You get to go Christmas shopping with Mom or Dad
26. You get to take the family out for pizza (Dad gets to pay!)
27. You get to attend a Christmas concert

CHRISTMAS "STOCKING STUFFERS"

Have each child hang their stocking on the wall or fireplace and then let them secretly draw the name of the family member's stocking which they are in charge of filling. The children will not be competing with the larger, more expensive gifts, which Santa will be bringing. Only small items, which can fit in the stocking, can be bought.

These items are easier to buy and often prove much more "practical" than many of the "throw away" presents often received at Christmas. For example, such items as chapstick, combs, etc. can be given, each present being individually wrapped. The children can purchase and wrap the gifts throughout the month as they earn money for them.

LETTERS TO SANTA

Save the letters that your children write to Santa each year. Put them in plastic page covers for preservation and place these in a three-ring binder.

Show them (or give them) to your child on a special Christmas...such as their first Christmas after marriage.

Dear Santa,
- Bicycle
- Ball
- Shirt
- Puppy
- Games
- Puzzle
- Skis
- Computer
- Coat
- Gloves
- Horse

SLEEPING AROUND THE CHIRSTMAS TREE

As a family, spend an evening putting up and decorating your Christmas tree together. As bedtime rolls around, have all the children bring a sleeping bag and pillow and place it by the tree.

The foot of their bags should be next to the tree so they can look at the tree while lying down. Turn out the living room lights, turn on some good Christmas music, and plug in the Christmas tree lights. Time for some truly sweet dreams....

DOOR DECORATING CONTEST

Early in December explain to the children that you are going to have a Christmas door-decorating contest. Each child can pick one door in the house and will be given one week in which to decorate it. Have lots of construction paper and glue available for their use, and check out some Christmas craft books from the library to help give them ideas of what they may want to make.

One evening about a week later, have Dad serve as judge. Make certain that prizes are given to everyone, so that **all** are "winners." The first place winner gets to choose his or her prize first, second place winner chooses next, and so on. Prizes might include a package of Oreo cookies, a bag of candy, etc.

A VISIT FROM SANTA

For making Christmas memories, one of the best investments a family can make is in the purchase of a Santa Claus suit. Dad will wear this, while the children can be Santa's helpers, wearing red Santa hats.

One evening, all dress up, jump in the car, and go on a visit to friends, family members, and neighbors. Ring the doorbell and be prepared with a carol or two as your friends answer the door. Santa's helpers can then give the children at the house you are visiting some candy and a holiday gift you have prepared for the occasion. As your children get older, let them take turns being Santa.

DINNER & BIRTHDAY CAKE FOR JESUS

While Santa seems to be the star of the show on Christmas morning, make certain that Christ is center stage the evening before. To set the proper mood, on Christmas Eve begin with a "Jerusalem dinner." All come to the dinner table dressed in Holy Land attire--bath robes can be worn over regular clothes and towels can be tied across the top of the head, hanging down over the neck. The meal should consist of fish, unleavened bread, fruits, and grape juice, just as Mary and Joseph might have had.

After dinner bring out a special birthday cake for Jesus, remembering that it truly is His birthday that we celebrate at Christmas. Take turns going around the table allowing each person to tell some "fact" about Jesus (such as: Jesus walked on the water; Jesus fed five thousand people using only a few fishes and loaves of bread; Jesus chose twelve apostles; Jesus was born in a manger; Jesus learned to be a carpenter from his earthly father, Joseph; etc.). As each person describes one "fact" they know about Jesus, they place a candle on His cake. When all of the candles have been put on the cake, they are lit, and the family sings "Happy Birthday" to Jesus.

CHRISTMAS PAJAMAS

Since children generally wear out a pair of pajamas within a year's time, a really fun tradition is to provide them with some new sleepwear each Christmas Eve. Make sure to wrap them up, so that just before bedtime they have the excitement of opening a present!

A NATIVITY VIDEO

    If you have a video camera available to you, a truly memorable experience is making your own home video movie of the nativity. First, find a good children's book which gives a good narrative of the nativity--or, using the Bible as a guide, make up your own script. Decide what scenes will be needed (and in what order), who will do the narrating, who the acting, and what, if any, spoken parts will be given.

    If you live in the country, or have friends who do, you might want to include some scenes of Mary actually sitting on a donkey (or horse), shepherds standing in a field (or corral) full of sheep, etc. Only the resources available to you...and your imagination limit your production. But even if shot entirely in your own living room, the event will be memorable for years to come if your family does it!

A GIFT FOR VISITORS

Similar to the Valentine's Day "Kiss" Countdown, as previously described, use gingerbread cookies to show your love and affection for those who visit your house during the Christmas season. Make gingerbread boys together as a family one evening. Cover with icing, using M&M's for eyes and buttons or use decorating icing that comes in plastic tubes that can be purchased at your local grocery store. Similar to the string of chocolate "Kisses" you made during Valentine's Day, lay a long strip of Handi-Wrap on your kitchen counter and place a line of gingerbread men down the middle of it. Fold the clear plastic over the cookies from both sides and separate the cookies by tying red ribbon between each.

Hang a string of the cookies on the wall, inside the house next to the front door. As visitors are leaving, have one of your children cut off a cookie and give it to them. When one string of cookies is gone, go to the freezer where you have stored those extra strings of cookies which have been impatiently waiting to be hung on the wall...cut down...and eaten!

YULE LOG

When disposing of your Christmas tree be sure to cut off the bottom 18 inches or so of the trunk and save it for next year. This will become your "Yule log." Bring it out on Christmas Eve and decorate it with red bows and pines cones (attach using hot wax). You may wish to go to the library and look up the history of "Yule logs" and read this to the children. Each person makes a wish just before the log is set afire in the stove or fireplace.

166

A FAMILY GIFT

While Santa should take care of the wants and needs of each individual child, make certain that a family gift is provided that all can use and that will promote family togetherness all year long. For example, a family-sized rubber raft, Ping-Pong table, family tent and camping equipment, etc. Books that can be read together as a family are also an extremely valuable gift.

CHRISTMAS TREE BURNING PARTY

The children are more willing to help you take down Christmas decorations and straighten up the house if they know that afterwards a special "tree burning" party will be held. Cut up the tree and light. Be prepared with hot dogs and marshmallows, ready to roast!

THANK YOU PARTY

A few days after Christmas get the family together and make "thank you" cards. (This is not really a "party," but if you call it that, the kids will think it's fun!) Send thank you's to all that gave gifts or dropped off treats. Have refreshments at the end, including special cookies which have a note attached, stating: "Smart cookies never forget to say thanks!"

FIRST DAY OF WINTER

Make the first day of winter (or the first snowfall) an opportunity to add a little fun to your evening meal. Have everyone find their winter hat, gloves or mittens, that they must wear throughout dinner. This will get you all in the spirit of the cold and harsh winter ahead!

COLUMBUS DAY

You can celebrate this holiday simply by fixing a **round** pizza, and discussing with your family how Columbus was one of the few in his day who was certain the world was round!

Here's a really fun Columbus Day menu. Prepare Spanish rice (since Columbus sailed from Spain); tossed salad with Italian dressing (since he was Italian); apple pie (because he sailed to America); and have your husband dress up like an Indian to serve the meal!

Make your family "Sloppy Joe Boats" for dinner. Here's the recipe:

1 lb. ground beef
1 small onion, chopped
1 can chicken gumbo soup
1/4 cup ketchup
1 large loaf of French bread

Directions: Cut French bread in half to serve open-faced, and top with fried ground beef mixture (using above ingredients). Add cheese on top, and melt in oven. Insert small dowel stick in each half of the bread and glue a small "sail" made from construction paper onto each stick. Then place the two "ships" on the dining room table along with an Italian salad.

GROUNDHOG'S DAY

A simple way to celebrate Groundhog's Day is to fix food that a Groundhog would love!

Prepare small "nibbling" items, such as: nuts, baby carrots, celery sticks with peanut butter, berries or raisins, any type of leafy vegetable, etc. If you want to really get crazy, put a few bowls of water out and let family members lap it up.

If time doesn't permit the preparation of a truly Groundhog's menu, simply fix your normal dinner, and eat it on the *ground* like a groundhog by just spreading a blanket on the living room floor.

For an after dinner activity, draw each family member's shadow. To do this use butcher paper or paper ends from the office of your local newspaper. Hang a long sheet of this paper on the wall and shine a light on it. In turn, have each family member stand in front of the paper, while other members trace their shadow on the paper. If time permits, using markers, crayons, etc., see who can make their shadow look the silliest!

HOLIDAY PILLOWCASES

Immediately following a holiday, go down to your local fabric store and buy holiday fabric. Use this to make special holiday pillow cases for each child in the family. Three-quarters of a yard of fabric will make one pillowcase. Let the children use their special pillowcase during the entire month in which the holiday occurs. These pillowcases are lightweight and take up very little room for packing. In later years, when a child is in college or away from home they can be used to help the child still feel part of the family during holidays.